W9-CMO-779

Financial
Forecasting
and
Planning

Recent Titles from Quorum Books

Decision Support Systems in Finance and Accounting
H. G. Heymann and Robert Bloom

Freedom of Speech on Private Property
Warren Freedman

Causes of Failure in Performance Appraisal and Supervision: A Guide to Analysis and Evaluation for Human Resource Professionals
Joe Baker, Jr.

The Modern Economics of Housing: A Guide to Theory and Policy for Finance and Real Estate Professionals
Randall Johnston Pozdena

Productivity and Quality through Science and Technology
Y. K. Shetty and Vernon M. Buehler, editors

Interactive Corporate Compliance: An Alternative to Regulatory Compulsion
Jay A. Sigler and Joseph Murphy

Voluntary Corporate Liquidations
Ronald J. Kudla

Business-Government Relations and Interdependence: A Managerial and Analytic Perspective
John M. Stevens, Steven L. Wartick, and John W. Bagby

Career Growth and Human Resource Strategies: The Role of the Human Resource Professional in Employee Development
Manuel London and Edward M. Mone, editors

Guide to International Real Estate Investment
M. A. Hines

Occupational Job Evaluation: A Research-Based Approach to Job Classification
Wilfredo R. Manese

The Professionals' Guide to Fund Raising, Corporate Giving, and Philanthropy: People Give to People
Lynda Lee Adams-Chau

FINANCIAL FORECASTING AND PLANNING

A Guide for Accounting, Marketing, and Planning Managers

Sharon Hatten Garrison,
Wallace N. Davidson, Jr.,
and
Michael A. Garrison

Quorum Books
NEW YORK · WESTPORT, CONNECTICUT · LONDON

Library of Congress Cataloging-in-Publication Data

Garrison, Sharon Hatten.
  Financial forecasting and planning : a guide for accounting.
marketing, and planning managers / Sharon Hatten Garrison, Wallace
N. Davidson, Jr., and Michael A. Garrison.
   p. cm.
Includes Index.
ISBN 0–89930–265–3 (lib. bdg. : alk. paper)
   1. Business enterprises—Finance. 2. Business forecasting.
I. Davidson, Wallace N. (Wallace Norman), 1952–   . II. Garrison,
Michael A. III. Title.
HG4026.G37   1988
658.1′5′—dc 19   87–36097

British Library Cataloguing in Publication Data is available.

Library of Congress Catalog Card Number: 87–36097
ISBN: 0–89930–265–3

First published in 1988 by Quorum Books

Greenwood Press, Inc.
88 Post Road West, Westport, Connecticut 06881

Printed in the United States of America

The paper used in this book complies with the
Permanent Paper Standard issued by the National
Information Standards Organization (Z39.48–1984).

10 9 8 7 6 5 4 3 2 1

The authors gratefully acknowledge the assistance of
Nancy Hyder, W. Joe Mason, Jr., and Lorna
Watkins. Thanks to all of them.

CONTENTS

Financial
Forecasting
and
Planning

1

INTRODUCTION

In the economic heyday of the late 1960s and early 1970s, the airline industry saw burgeoning consumer interest, increasing technology, and, best of all, regulated markets. On the whole, the industry was flying high (pun intended). Braniff was perhaps one of the more notable companies in the airline industry during this period. Notable, perhaps, in retrospect—for Braniff was to become the biggest company (until that time) to declare bankruptcy. Braniff decided to become the highest of the high flyers. It invested in designer uniforms for flight attendants, painted its planes purple, and sought out new routes to fly. The company went heavily into debt in order to finance such moves. During the same era, some airline companies (such as Southwest Airlines) opted for a more conservative approach. They planned for a more "managed" growth. Eventually, with deregulation and increased fuel prices, Braniff's empire collapsed. Many look at this story and feel compassion for Braniff. After all, who could have foreseen deregulation, oil embargoes, labor problems, and the like.

In the early 1980s Texas oil companies were on the move, in part because of one of the disasters that touched Braniff: the oil embargo. The oil embargo led to increased energy prices. This cost Braniff millions in operating costs, but it meant big dollars in sales to the Texas oil companies. Texas banks were waiting in line to lend these companies money. Pretty soon the banks had nice balance sheets and returns to show off. Unfortunately, many of these same banks did not plan for their course of action should oil revenues fall. When they started falling, many of the oil companies defaulted on their loans, leading to the failure of some banks in petroleum states. Many might look at this situation and feel sorry for the banks. Who could have foreseen the huge collapse in oil prices and all the attendant problems?

Perhaps no company could have foreseen all these circumstances. The question that should be asked, though, is why these companies did not have some sort of strategy for what they would do *just in case* any of these circumstances did occur. Successful companies *plan*.

PLANNING

Most "average" managers marvel at how some "lucky" people are always in the right place at the right time; but being in the right place at the right time is usually a matter of planning. A good planner makes the place and the time.

Planning is usually the key to success, not only for individuals but for businesses as well. Trying to predict future events and working out contingency strategies is one key to a successful company. A first-rate company tries to visualize different circumstances that may arise in the future and works out several alternate plans of action should these events occur.

It is surprising how many companies never develop any plans for the future. They have no idea what actions to take when circumstances change. Companies with good planning strategies can minimize damage should unfortunate events such as economic downturns, labor problems, or liquidity crunches occur. Likewise, companies with good planning strategies can seize the opportunities that might arise. If there is an opportunity to move into a new market, a company needs to know if it has the resources to proceed. If so, what will be the basis for deciding the potential of such a venture? Where will the money come from? What effect will such a move have on existing operations? How will stockholders view the decision? The company with a good planning strategy has already examined the answers to such questions. It has a plan of action and simply puts it into effect. The "average" company, on the other hand, may not even know where to begin to make effective decisions. By the time it figures out where to begin, someone else has seized the golden opportunity.

Tax changes are a prime example of how companies plan for different circumstances. Many companies at this date are trying to fathom the latest tax laws and seeking advice on how best to deal with new laws. The really first-rate companies don't wait. They followed the changes in tax laws as they developed. They examined all the proposals and all the different versions of changes. They forecast what effect such proposals would have on their companies' operations. Then they developed strategies on how to minimize adverse effects of proposed changes and they even started trying to find ways to profit from tax law changes. They looked at all possible scenarios. Of course not all the proposals would be adopted and certainly their final form would be different from the proposals. The point is that such companies are prepared, no matter what comes to pass. The more poorly prepared companies do not figure out what to do with tax law changes until it is too late. By the time they develop strategies, the laws may be revised yet again.

IMPORTANCE OF FORECASTING FINANCIAL STATEMENTS

Forecasting financial statements is an essential ingredient in a successful planning program. Forecasted statements illustrate the bottom line of different financial scenarios. The statements are useful in predicting the effect of ordinary business influences. There are a number of other reasons why forecasted financial statements are important: (1) They are helpful in aiding a firm in the determination of its financing requirements; (2) they are useful in making investment decisions; and (3) they allow managers to "try on" different strategies by gauging their effect on different financial variables.

OTHERS WHO USE FINANCIAL STATEMENTS

Forecasts are crucial to successful managers, but there are other audiences interested in forecasting financial statements. Potential creditors certainly need to be familiar with the basics of planning and forecasting. In assessing whether to loan money to someone or to some company, creditors need to be familiar with the present and future financial situation of potential borrowers. By applying the basics of financial statement forecasting, creditors can better gauge a potential borrower's future. Investors and stockholders also need to be familiar with the basics of forecasting financial statements. Certainly before anyone advances any dollars into a potential investment, they would want to assess the future of that investment. This book will be beneficial in learning the basics of forecasting that future.

OVERVIEW OF THE FORECASTING PROCESS

If a company were attempting to predict its position a year from now, the projected balance sheet would be the most important piece of information to assess that position. The balance sheet is a detail of what the company owns (assets), what the company owes (liabilities), and the difference between the two (equity). For an example, see Table 1.1. By showing this "own-owe" position, the balance sheet is a measure of a company's financial health. It is important to gauge the financial health of the firm at the end of the planning period. The object of the forecasting process is to project what the balance sheet will look like a year from now, as illustrated in Figure 1.1.

How would someone get from here to there? How can someone take today's balance sheet and get to tomorrow's balance sheet? What are the factors that will determine the changes in the balance sheet? Where should someone start? To get straight to the point, the determination of the coming year's sales is the place to start. Sales affect production, inventory, cash, accounts receivable, and so on. Everything else involved in the planning process will depend on what the company's sales will be.

Table 1.1
Delta Company 19X1 Balance Sheet

Cash	$ 20,000	Accounts Payable	$ 10,000
Marketable Securitites	10,000	Accruals	4,000
Receivables	50,000	Notes Payable @ 10%	24,000
Inventory	70,000	Total	$ 38,000
Total	$150,000	Long-term Debt @ 15%	96,000
Net Fixed Assets	160,000	Common Stock	64,000
		Retained Earnings	112,000
Total Assets	$310,000	Total	$310,000

Other Selected Data:

Sales	$200,000
Net Income	10,000
Dividends	4,000

The first step in the forecasting process is to generate a sales forecast. There are a number of methods for forecasting sales, and some are covered in Chapter 2. Once a good sales forecast exists, it may be coupled with an analysis of inventory to make up a production plan. Armed with the production plan and a historical analysis of costs, an income statement can be generated. Then cash budgets, capital budgets, and other supporting budgets may be drawn. The final step in the process involves taking the beginning balance sheet and all the other statements that have been formulated in the planning process and combining elements to form the projected balance sheet. A model of the process might be illustrated in the fashion described in Figure 1.2.

The forecasting process is extensive and somewhat time-consuming, but it will allow the management of the company to ask (and answer) questions about the key planning factors in the coming financial period. Unless all the right questions are addressed, the company may not be fully prepared for contingencies. As elaborated upon in later chapters, these questions and plans are probably the most important factors in the planning process. The mere formulation of budgets and statements is secondary to the process. It will be seen that these budgets and statements are a guide to the process and not the objective. The real objective of the planning process is to ask questions, formulate strategies, and look at all the issues.

Different companies go about planning in different ways. Take a hypothetical company, Alpha. Alpha figures it needs to make budgets at the end of the year. It emphasizes that budgets and forecasted statements be as accurate as possible. However, Alpha feels that it just does not have the management time to spend

Figure 1.1
Balance Sheets for Two Years

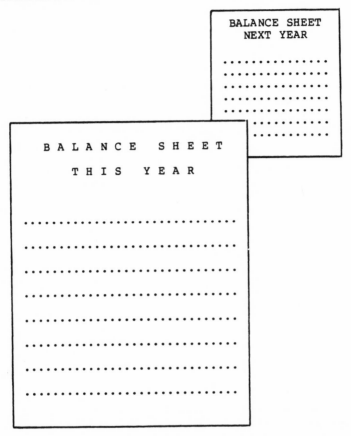

a great deal of effort on the planning process. It emphasizes shortcut methods and has even devised some computer programs to cut down the time spent on development of budgets and statements. Alpha points with pride to the fact that for the past five years figures on its pro forma statements came within 5 percent of actual statements at the end of the planning process.

A second company, Delta, does not favor the shortcut methods. It spends the extra time going through the full-blown planning process. Delta's predictive accuracy on forecasted statements does not even come close to Alpha's. Its projected statements come only within 13 percent of actual statements at the end of the planning process. Yet because it spent the extra time Delta did the following:

1. It arranged a line of credit with the bank. Delta knew it would have a couple of months with cash shortfalls, so it went ahead and worked out an arrangement with the bank.

In doing so, it was able to strike a favorable agreement and got a good rate of financing. Delta figures it was able to save 1.25 percent on all the money it would have to borrow over the next year.

2. Delta found that a drill press was nearing the end of its productive life and it would have to replace the equipment sometime during the next year. Instead of waiting until the equipment broke down, Delta started "shopping" immediately. The best piece of equipment was found and delivery was arranged at a convenient time. By shopping early, Delta figures it saved as much as $38,000 by not having to buy from the vendor who could supply the equipment immediately.

3. Delta found in its projections that it would have a couple of months where it would

Figure 1.2
An Overview of the Forecasting Process

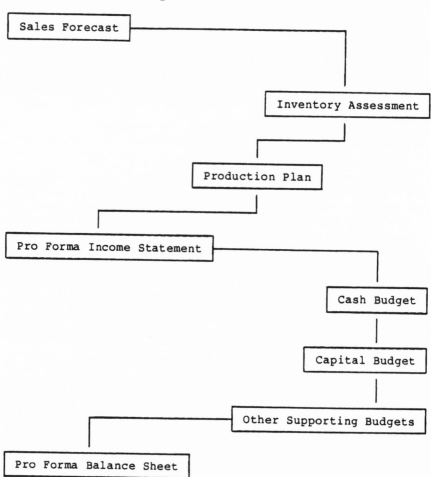

be pressed on its production schedule. Estimates were made of how much overtime would cost and it was decided instead to job out part of the load to an outside company, saving $12,000.

It is obvious that Delta is probably more successful in planning than Alpha. Sure, its projected statements might not be as accurate, but it fulfilled its objective. The objective again is not the *statements* but the *plans*.

SHORTCUT METHODS

There is no substitute for a full-blown forecasting process. However, management time is often at a premium. There are shortcut methods available for planning, but because they may not address all the questions desired, they should not be considered a substitute for the comprehensive planning process described in Figure 1.2, but rather as a supplement. One helpful shortcut method is described in Chapter 4.

GETTING STARTED

It is now obvious that good planning is important. A guideline to follow is already known. Figure 1.2 illustrates the planning process; but getting started may not be so easy. Unfortunately there are no hard and fast rules on how to begin. What each manager does is contingent on the individual situation. For instance, the size of the company will have an impact on the planning process. A one-person company does not have to worry about meetings, personalities, and the like. A large company has to worry about getting many people involved.

Another factor that must be considered is whether or not a planning process is already in place. If so, the manager may need to review what is already in place and determine if modifications are necessary. If there is no existing structure, then one must be started. Regardless, the objectives of what the manager is trying to accomplish should be established as early as possible. In a large company, many will be involved in various stages of the planning process. At this point it is useful to see who some of these personnel are and what duties they might perform in the planning process.

PERSONNEL IN THE PLANNING PROCESS

A number of personnel will play parts in the planning process. Not all companies will have different individuals filling these slots, but someone will have to fulfill all the duties. Sometimes companies have only a controller who has to fulfill all the planning duties as well as those of the financial manager. Sometimes a company will have only one marketing specialist who will act as marketing manager and marketing research director. Among the key players involved in the planning process are: financial manager, controller, production manager, cash manager, receivables manager, purchasing director, marketing manager, and marketing research manager. This is not necessarily an all-inclusive list of duties, but rather a general guide.

Financial Manager. Integral to the planning process, the financial manager will play a part in many instances. It is the financial manager who will oversee the financing decisions, such as arranging for lines of credit, determining the need for longer-term sources of credit, and deciding upon what sources of credit should be used. In addition, the financial manager will project what effect plans and forecasted situations will have on stockholder relations. The financial manager will work in close harmony with the controller or accounting manager in drawing up and analyzing budgets and forecasted statements.

Controller. The controller should oversee the actual formulation of budgets and statements and in concert with the financial manager should aid in the analysis of such statements.

Production Manager. The production manager will make estimated production schedules. In doing so, the production manager will make inventory decisions, look at projected expenditures for labor, materials, and overhead. One important duty of the production manager should be to review the status of machinery and equipment. This is the time to determine if all the equipment is "healthy." If not, replacement, repair, or leasing of other equipment should be explored.

Cash Manager. The cash manager obviously will work with the cash budgets and cash flow statements of the company. Most generally, the cash manager will work under the auspices of the controller or the accounting manager.

Receivables Manager. The accounts receivables manager will examine past collections experience of the company to provide estimates of accounts receivables collection for the planning period in order to estimate both accounts receivables and cash flows.

Purchasing Manager. The purchasing manager or director will make estimates of materials costs for the forecasting period. This is also a good opportunity to assess vendor relations, look at purchasing procedures, update contracts, examine new price schedules, and the like.

Marketing Manager. The marketing manager will work with sales forecasts, estimate selling and advertising costs, review personnel needs for sales function, and such related functions.

Marketing Research Manager. The marketing research manager is responsible for the formulation of sales forecasts.

No mention has been made about which individual should be in charge of the planning process. In many companies it is natural for the financial manager to assume control of the process; but in some cases this would not work. Again, the model is dependent on each individual situation.

Using the stages that were described in Figure 1.2, Figure 1.3 shows some of the personnel who may become involved in each stage of the process. The figure also illustrates some of the issues that should be addressed in each stage. Chapter 3 will cover in depth all the steps outlined. It is important to keep in mind that many of the key personnel involved in the process may also be novices at planning. A good planning process requires experience and training, but everyone has to start somewhere.

At times it may be exasperating to deal with inexperienced personnel, but time spent now pays benefits in the evolution of the process. Another thing to keep in mind is that even an "expert" in financial matters may have had minimal exposure to planning. Because little time may be spent on financial planning in business school curricula, even Certified Public Accountants, financial managers, and bankers may not have all the necessary tools to institute a top-notch planning process. Chapter 10 provides some sources of information on how to gear up for planning.

Figure 1.3
Stages in the Planning Process

I: SALES FORECAST

Personnel	Issues
Financial Manager	Sales in Units
Controller	Pricing
Marketing Manager	Economic Outlook
Marketing Research Director	Raw Materials Sources
	Timing of Sales

II: INVENTORY ASSESSMENT

Personnel	Issues
Financial Manager	Inventory Check For Fitness
Purchasing	Inventory Flow
	Start Assessing Labor Outlook

III: PRODUCTION PLAN

Personnel	Issues
Production Manager	Check on Equipment
Purchasing	Labor Relations
	Materials Flow
	Production Scheduling

IV: PRO FORMA INCOME STATEMENT

Personnel	Issues
Financial Manager	Costs and Expenses
Controller	Tax Planning
	Profit Considerations
	Stockholder Relations

Figure 1.3—Continued

V: CASH BUDGET

Personnel	Issues
Financial Manager Controller Cash Manager	Cash Forecasting Cash Flow Management Short Term Financing Considerations

VI: CAPITAL BUDGET

Personnel	Issues
Financial Manager Controller Cash Manager Production Manager	Equipment Planning Investments Planning Long-Term Financing Considerations

VII: OTHER SUPPORTING BUDGETS

Personnel	Issues
Financial Manager Controller	

VIII: PRO FORMA BALANCE SHEET

Personnel	Issues
Financial Manager Controller	Stockholder Relations Creditor Relations Resource Planning

NOTE: This model is only a suggestion for a possible check-
list in the planning process. It is not all-
inclusive. Each individual situation may dictate
a different model. The model also does not reflect
the fact that some individual or committee must
orchestrate the entire process.

DESIGN OF THIS BOOK

This book is designed so that someone with a rudimentary knowledge of
accounting can follow it quite easily. It is primarily aimed at managers, although
it may be useful for creditors, investors, and accounting professionals. It is not
intended as a complete manual detailing the total planning process. Rather, it is

a techniques-oriented guide outlining the construction of forecasted statements.

This chapter serves as an introductory chapter and outlines some of the personnel who might be involved in the planning process. Chapter 2 shows some techniques for forecasting sales. Chapter 3 introduces a fundamental model for forecasting statements, complete with easy-to-follow examples. Chapter 4 outlines a shortcut method for forecasting financial statements. Chapters 5, 6, and 7 provide managers with some practical applications of the fundamental model. A discussion of ratio analysis of forecasted statements and a discussion of growth implications are provided. Chapter 8 presents an advanced model. Chapter 9 shows how computers can aid in the process of forecasting. A detailed example of forecasting statements using electronic spreadsheet programs is covered. Chapter 10 offers sources of assistance to the planner and cautions to be observed in the planning process. The appendixes contain a "Basic" program for forecasting statements and a list of industry sources.

2

FORECASTING SALES

As already mentioned, sales is the one business variable that will affect the outcome of a company over the ensuing financial period more than any other variable. It is the cornerstone of financial planning and should therefore be approached quite carefully. However, it should also be kept in mind that the purpose of sales forecasting is not to forecast sales with pinpoint accuracy. Rather it is to come up with a reasonable sales forecast that will start the ball rolling and allow planners to ask and answer necessary questions. In other words, don't get so carried away with devising the sales forecast that all the other steps in the planning process are forgotten.

For some companies a sales forecast is easy. For instance, a defense contractor with only one customer and contracts already in hand can predict sales over the next financial period with relative ease. The manufacturer of a completely new and revolutionary product will have a pretty tough time predicting what sales will be. For that reason not all companies can use the same approach in forecasting sales. There are a number of techniques available for forecasting sales, each with its own advantages and disadvantages. The objective of any sales forecast is to aid a company in planning its purchases, personnel, finances, and production levels.

The first thing a company should decide is whether to let a marketing research company or some outside consultant forecast sales. The alternative is in-house sales forecasting. The next thing to decide is what sales forecasting technique to adopt. This chapter outlines some of the major sales forecasting techniques with relevant characteristics. This is not a primer in the techniques, however. A "how-to" in sales forecasting is a book in itself. Rather, this chapter is only a guide to the manager in talking to the sales forecasting professionals. Following the description of each of the techniques is an outline of some considerations in the selection of which technique to use.

IN-HOUSE SALES FORECASTING VERSUS OUTSIDE CONSULTANTS

The first decision to be made in sales forecasting is whether to do the job in-house or to use some outside consultant or marketing research firm. The answer depends on the resources of the company. First of all, does the company have trained personnel in the company qualified to do the job? Does the company have an adequate information base to use in sales forecasting? How accurate must the forecast be, and how efficiently can available personnel achieve that accuracy? Last, what financial resources does the company have? Even if the company feels it needs to use an outside consultant, if it doesn't have the money then it will have to look to other sources—consultants don't come cheap. On the other hand, because of experience they can minimize the time spent on a sales forecast and are often less expensive to use than might be imagined.

In deciding whether to use an outside consultant, there are a number of things a manager might keep in mind. First of all, inventory available resources. A company may already have adequate and trained personnel in place. Then the next step is to estimate needed accuracy of any sales forecast. If pinpoint accuracy is crucial, then outside help may be more important in achieving that accuracy. It is also wise to check the cost of outside consultants. It might be that the cost is reasonable enough when compared to time expenditures of in-house personnel that a manager will decide to use outside help anyway. It is also possible that the cost is reasonable enough to use as a check against in-house sales forecasts. If a company decides to use an outside consultant, it would be wise to talk with professional associates and the like to check references. A number of directories are available from industry and trade groups listing marketing research firms in different geographical areas. Most are available at larger public libraries.

SALES FORECASTING METHODS

Once the manager has decided on whether to go in-house or outside, then the method of sales forecasting must be decided. There are a number of methods available; most fall within three general categories: (1) qualitative or judgmental methods, (2) time series methods, and (3) causal methods.

Qualitative or Judgmental Methods

There are several qualitative or judgmental methods that may be used in sales forecasting. These methods are subjective and are used when: (1) low cost methods are needed, (2) there is a scarcity of data, (3) the company has stable sales volume, (4) there is little chance of serious error, (5) errors have little serious implication, and/or (6) managers have depth of experience in the firm. The types of qualitative/judgmental methods are case history, executive judg-

ments, supercommittees, artificial intelligence, sales goals, and best-guess forecasts.

Case history or historical analogy types of techniques base forecasts on comparisons to similar products or successes/failures of the past. Generally, such
techniques are used in new product introduction. The accuracy of such techniques
varies, but the expense is moderate.

Example: Delta is thinking about introducing a new stereo cabinet. The last
time it introduced a line of audio furniture, sales were quite low the first year
following introduction, but there was a definite upward trend around Christmas.
Based on these historical results, Delta might forecast sales for the new stereo
cabinet utilizing the historical trends.

Executive judgments are based on intuitive judgments of key executives. Such
judgments may not be as inaccurate as might be imagined. Key executives may
have well-developed skills based on experience and knowledge of the firm.
Executive judgment techniques might be used in conjunction with other methods
in developing sales forecasts. These techniques are simple and inexpensive.
Drawbacks are that such methods place a great deal of emphasis on "opinions"
and such opinions may be misplaced; also such techniques may take up valuable
executive time.

Example: The general manager for Delta Company has worked for the company for the past 25 years in various capacities. He is generally regarded by
competitors as the most knowledgeable manager in the industry. Based on the
insight gained from these years of experience, the general manager puts together
a sales forecast. In doing so, he intuitively brings together his knowledge of his
product, his industry, his customer base, and the economy.

Supercommittees might be formed to put together the views of a group of
experts. There are a number of ways this might be instituted, but the goal is to
converge toward a common group estimate. An advantage is that the group
prohibits one person from forcing individual opinions on the sales forecast.
Accuracy can be quite good, but the obvious expense in time is quite high.

Example: Delta puts together a committee of experts which includes the sales
manager, product managers for the various lines, the general manager, and
similar experts. The first committee meeting allows these experts to put forward
in the form of an anonymous questionnaire their own individual ideas on what
Delta's sales forecast will be. The next committee meeting airs the results of
the previous questionnaire. Committee members are given the opportunity to
comment on the information. A new questionnaire will be completed. This
process continues until a consensus results or until members reach the point
where they decide to take a statistical average of results.

New generations of computers have resulted in *artificial intelligence* ap-
proaches to forecasting. These computers allow the input of managers, which
is used to program the computers into making decisions similar to those the
manager would have made. This is a relatively new technology and has a great
deal of promise. At present, though, such techniques are quite expensive.

Example: Delta contracts with a consulting firm specializing in artifical intelligence. Delta's general manager (the one with all the experience and knowledge) sits down with a representative of the consulting firm. He is interviewed extensively about what he does and how he looks at various decisions. The objective of all this probing is eventually to model all the factors that go into his decision making. Using the new artificial intelligence technology, the consulting firm programs the results. Supposedly there is a program available to Delta that *thinks* like the general manager. From now on, the program will be utilized in sales forecasting (and perhaps other decisions as well).

Sales goals result when management of the company dictates goals to be achieved by the company. This is a sort of "top-down" approach. Figure 2.1 illustrates the idea behind this technique. There are a number of factors to consider in using sales goals: (1) sales goals must be consistent with overall corporate objectives; (2) a reward structure must be provided; (3) sales goals must be realistic; and (4) management must consider market forces at work.

A *best-guess forecast* is a sort of bottoms-up type of forecast. The sales force, based upon customer contact and input, forwards forecasts up channels and modifications occur at channels. This idea is illustrated in Figure 2.2.

Time Series Methods

Time series methods are used to obtain forecasts by using historical quantitative data. Elements considered may include seasonal variations, secular trends, and cyclical trends. Types of time series methods include trend analysis, moving average, exponential smoothing, and Box-Jenkins methods.

Figure 2.1
Sales Goals

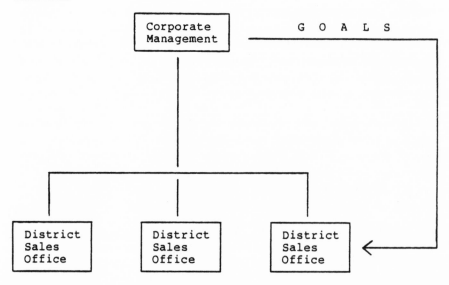

Figure 2.2
The Best-Guess Forecast

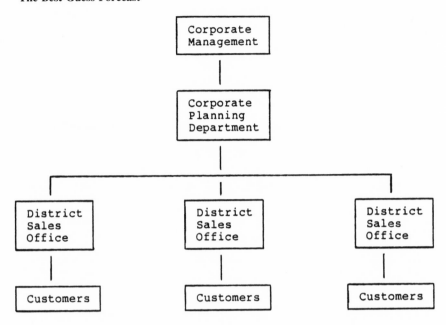

Trend analysis techniques are common statistical sales forecasting techniques that forecast future sales based on recent patterns. These techniques simply fit a trend line into a mathematical equation and then project the line into the future. Trend lines can be cyclical, constant, or consistent. Figure 2.3 illustrates such trend lines.

Trend analysis is simple and accurate in stable industries, but the analysis does not consider economic decline, change in consumer habits, or improved technology. A number of observations are required in order to identify any trend. The accuracy of trend analysis can be quite good, especially for products in middle stages of their life cycle.

There are a number of ways of going about a trend analysis. Among the methods of calculating a trend are to calculate (1) a point-to-point estimate of compound growth, (2) an average point-to-point estimate, and (3) a regression approach.

1. A point-to-point estimate of compound growth is achieved by picking an appropriate number of years and estimating the compounded growth rate from one point to another. For an example refer to Table 2.1, which shows a history of sales for Delta Company. The sales history begins with $100,000 and ends with $168,000. To find a compound growth rate, calculate "g," the growth rate shown in the Table 2.2. Solving the equation results in a growth rate of 6.7 percent. To find a 1986 sales estimate, take 1985 sales, $168,000, and add 6.7 percent to it. As shown in the table the resulting sales estimate will be $179,256.

Figure 2.3
Trend Lines

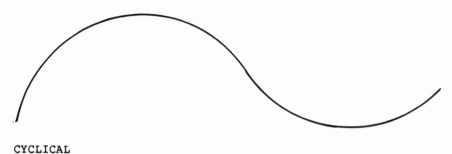

CYCLICAL

CONSTANT

CONSISTENT

Table 2.1
Sales History, Delta Company

YEAR	SALES ($)
1977	100,000
1978	110,000
1979	119,000
1980	128,000
1981	138,000
1982	147,000
1983	155,000
1984	162,000
1985	168,000

Table 2.2
Forecasting Sales: Compound Growth

Year	Sales ($)	
1977	100,000	
1978	110,000	A point-to-point estimate
1979	119,000	picks an appropriate
1980	128,000	number of years and
1981	138,000	estimates the compounded
1982	147,000	growth rate from one
1983	155,000	point to another.
1984	162,000	
1985	168,000	

Point-to-Point Estimate:

$$100,000 \ (1 + g)^8 \ = \ 168,000$$

$$(1 + g)^8 \ = \ 1.680$$

$$g \quad = \ 6.7\%$$

Some of the problems encountered will be picking the number of years to be used and the problems of varying growth rates. These must be solved by the judgment of the executive. The problem of varying growth rates might be solved by using an average point-to-point method.

2. An average point-to-point method will provide a consistent answer with point-to-point calculations when both points are realistic. For instance, refer again to Table 2.1. Note there are nine years. Suppose the analyst divided these up into the blocks of three years each. The average sales for the first block could be found by summing $100,000, $110,000, and $119,000 and then dividing by three. The average sales that would result would be $109,667. Likewise the average sales for the last block would be $161,667. Refer to Table 2.3 to see this. The growth rate that solves the compound growth equation is 6.7 percent, exactly what was found in the previous example. Of course, it is recognized that if different years and different blocks are used, different rates of growth may result. Again, what is chosen depends on the judgment of the executive performing the analysis. A separate problem might be involved in trying to predict rates of growth for a firm going through different phases of maturity. This notion is covered later in this chapter (section entitled "Forecasting in Different Maturity Phases").

3. A regression approach involves identifying causal variables and from past history computing a regression equation. For example, assume that a lumber company sells most of its product to homebuilders. Therefore, it is logical to assume that housing starts affect sales. Refer to Table 2.4 to see a past history

Table 2.3
Forecasting Sales: Compound Growth Based on Average Sales

Year	Sales ($)	Average Sales
1977	100,000 ⎤	
1978	110,000 ⎬	$109,667
1979	119,000 ⎦	
1980	128,000	
1981	138,000	
1982	147,000	
1983	155,000 ⎤	
1984	162,000 ⎬	$161,667
1985	168,000 ⎦	

Average Point-to-Point Estimate:

$$109{,}667 \ (1 + g)^6 = 161{,}667$$

$$(1 + g)^6 = 1.4742$$

$$g = 6.7\%$$

1986 Sales Estimate: $168,000 (1.067) = $179,256

of housing starts and sales. A graph plotting these points might be constructed as in Figure 2.4. The equation for the line drawn in Figure 2.4 is shown at the bottom of the figure. The result shows that the company has a base sales amount of $117,000. This amount is not dependent upon homebuilders, and tends not to vary. In addition to this $117,000, the company expects to achieve 9.74 (in 000s) times the amount of housing starts. In other words, if housing starts are predicted to be 30, the company should expect $409,200 in sales ($117 + 9.74(30) in 000s of dollars).

Moving averages are similar to trend analyses except that with moving averages earlier periods are dropped as later periods are added; this smooths out irregular influences in the past. These techniques are especially good for stable company sales. Disadvantages are that moving averages are useful only in the short run, seasonal or irregular periods of sales are not considered, and many periods are required in order to obtain the smoothing effect.

Exponential smoothing weights most recent data the heaviest since these data serve as better predictors of the future. It is better used when there is no appreciable trend or seasonal pattern. Forecasting accuracy can be very good in the short term. These techniques suffer from the same disadvantages as moving average techniques, however.

Box-Jenkins models utilize complex mathematical modeling to test different time series for best fit. These models try to account for repeated movements in

Table 2.4
Forecasting Sales: Regression Approach

The QuickMart Lumber Company sells about 75% of its total
sales to home builders.   In each quarter of the year, the
number of housing starts influences that quarter's sales.   A
past history of this phenomenon is presented below.

Quarter	($000) Sales	Housing Starts
1	430	30
2	335	21
3	520	35
4	490	42
5	470	37
6	210	20
7	195	8
8	270	17
9	400	35
10	480	25

historical series, be they trends, seasonal movements, or cyclical fluctuations.
Such techniques require substantial data and are quite time-consuming. Examples
involve statistical modeling and will not be explained in detail. Generally, the
use of such techniques is performed by someone other than the manager of the
company, be it a marketing research firm, programmer, or statistician. For more
details on any of these techniques, check the references at the end of this chapter.

Causal Methods

The causal methods are similar to the time series techniques in that they require
historical quantitative data. These techniques are used to find relationships between sales and other factors such as economic or social factors. Causal methods
include regression models, econometric models, and market surveys.

Regression models relate sales to economic, competitive, or internal variables
to come up with equations for prediction. A simplified regression example was
given in the discussion of trend analyses. Only one independent variable was

Figure 2.4
QuickMart Lumber Company

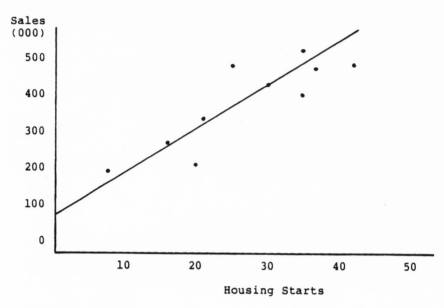

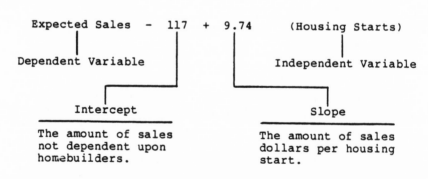

involved. More complicated regression models are frequently used in practice, some involving hundreds of independent variables. No specific example is given of this more complicated regression model. Again, for more detailed information, check one of the references at the end of the chapter.

Econometric models use a system of interdependent regression equations to describe an area of business activity in order to forecast changes in sales. This involves estimating changes in other areas (such as economic fluctuations).

Example: In the past, Delta built an econometric model detailing how its sales vary with economic changes. Given economic changes in the national economy, the furniture industry will vary and Delta's own company outcome will vary. Once the model is constructed, then Delta will forecast economic changes regularly with the objective of determining how such economic changes will impact on its own individual sales.

Market surveys measure intentions of consumers. Sampling of consumers can be expensive. It must also be remembered that consumer intention does not necessarily equate to consumer action.

Example: Delta contracts a marketing research company (although it could do the work itself) to survey a sample of potential customers. In this case, customers will fill out a questionnaire surveying their intentions to purchase furniture, of what kind, at what price, and the like. Based on results, a sales forecast for Delta will result.

FORECASTING IN DIFFERENT MATURITY PHASES

It is reasonable to assume that many companies will go through different phases of growth in their history. Take, for example, a biomedical company that is currently working to discover a cure for cancer. During the early phases, the company will be expending resources on research and development. Without any product lines, growth is sure to be slow. It may even be nonexistent or negative.

Should the company actually discover a cure for cancer, though, and should that cure reach the marketplace, there should be a tremendous explosion in growth. More than likely, most current cancer patients would clamor for the cure. Sooner or later, though, most of the existing patients would be cured and would no longer require the company's product. When that point is reached, the company's market is close to saturation. It can still look forward to selling its product to people who will develop cancer (unless someone discovers a prevention for the disease), but the rate of the company's growth will slow down. This might be described as the maturity phase of the company.

How should the company go about forecasting sales in such a situation? This company, because of the tremendous market involved, will have financial resources at its disposal and would probably want to employ the services of a reliable market research firm and perhaps undertake extensive market surveys throughout different maturity phases. A smaller company, or one without substantial resources at its disposal, will have to rely on other means. A simple (although most likely not as accurate as a good market survey) method is to estimate the rate of change in the company's growth rate.

For example, assume a small computer company has the sales history depicted in Table 2.5. The company realizes that the market for its product has become relatively saturated. Decision makers in the firm feel that peak growth in the company was typified by the period 1978–79, which was 12.6 percent. (This figure was arrived at by subtracting 1978 sales [$37.3 million] from 1979 sales

Table 2.5
Sales History

Year	Sales-- In Millions ($)
1978	37.3
1979	42.0
1980	46.6
1981	52.3
1982	55.9
1983	61.8
1984	68.2
1985	76.5
1986	84.5
1987	90.0
1988	94.7

[$42 million] and dividing the result by $37.3 million.) Although the decision makers feel that the company's sales will continue to grow, the rate of growth will be at a declining rate. They note that the rate of growth between 1987 and 1988 was only 5.2 percent ($94.7 million minus $90 million divided by $90 million). The company then estimates the rate of change in growth to be a negative 9.4 percent. (Refer to Table 2.6 for these calculations.)

To find the estimated rate of growth for 1989 the company takes the 1987–88 rate of growth, then modifies for the decline associated with maturity. It arrives at an estimate of 4.71 percent. Based on this estimate it arrives at forecasted 1989 sales as $99.16 million.

This illustration shows some of the concerns faced by managers when dealing with company growth. For additional growth considerations, refer to Chapter 7.

SELECTION OF A MODEL

There are a number of factors to be considered in the selection of a sales forecasting model. Among these considerations are the amount of accuracy required, the amount of money to spend, the amount of time between forecasts,

Table 2.6
Calculations

I. 1978-79 Growth Rate

$$\frac{42.0 - 37.3}{37.3} = 12.6\%$$

II. 1987-88 Growth Rate

$$\frac{94.7 - 90.0}{90.0} = 5.2\%$$

III. Rate of Change in Growth

$$12.6\% \ (1 + R)^9 = 5.2\%$$

$$R = -9.4\%$$

IV. Estimate for 1988-89 Growth Rate

$$g = 5.2\% \ (1 - .094) = 4.71\%$$

V. Estimate for 1989 Sales

$$1989 \ Sales = \$94.7(1.0471) = \$99.16$$

and the availability of data. Again, the selection of a method will depend on each individual situation. To overcome the weaknesses of some methods and to build on strengths of others, managers should consider using multiple or combined methods.

REFERENCES

Buell, Victor P. *Handbook of Modern Marketing*. New York: McGraw Hill, 1986, pp. 41-1 to 41-8.

Cox, James E., and Vithala R. Rao. *Sales Forecasting Methods: A Survey of Recent Developments*. Cambridge, Mass.: Marketing Science Institute, December 1978.

Eby, Frank H. *Sales Analysis Concepts & Applications*. New York: AMR International, Inc., 1982.

Evans, Joel R., and Berry Berman. *Marketing*. New York: Macmillan, 1982.

Gaideke, Ralph M., and Dennis H. Tootelian. *Marketing Principles & Applications*. Los Angeles: West Publishing Co., 1983.

Mohn, N. Carroll, and Lester C. Sartorius. *Sales Forecasting Models: A Diagnostic Approach*. Atlanta: Publishing Service Division, College of Business Administration, Georgia State University, 1976.

Neidell, Lester A. *Strategic Marketing Management*. Tulsa: Penn Well Publishing Co., 1983.

Sales Forecasting. New York: The Conference Board, 1978.

____ 3 ____

THE FORECASTING PROCESS

This chapter illustrates the steps, statements, and procedures in the entire forecasting process, once the sales forecast is completed. The important objective in all this is not the formulations of the actual statements, but rather the questions that arise during the process. Managers review such factors as the state of equipment, what to do if labor unrest threatens, and how to plan for cash shortfalls. By addressing potential problems, managers may devise contingency plans on how to deal with situations that might occur during the next planning period.

DETAILED SALES FORECASTS

Once a company has formulated a good sales forecast for the financial period, it should break down the sales forecast into months. This assures that the company will better predict those when sales are good and those when sales are poor. This breakdown is important because it allows management to plan for slack periods and peak periods. This affects production scheduling, inventory planning, labor considerations, cash forecasting, and the like. Using past data or market survey techniques a company might identify these monthly patterns. An example based on Delta Company might appear as in Tables 3.1–3.5. Obviously Delta is a seasonal sales company. This breakdown by months is important because it will impact on cash planning, production planning, and the like. A graph illustrating the seasonal fluctuations appears in Figure 3.1. This shows that Delta has its big sales in the first four months of the year, but it has slow periods throughout the remainder of the year.

Table 3.1
Sales Forecast—Annual

Cabinets	800 at	$200	$160,000
Chairs	1600 at	25	40,000
Desks	200 at	150	30,000
Benches	500 at	20	10,000
TOTAL SALES FOR YEAR			$240,000

INVENTORY ASSESSMENT

Delta is at the stage when it needs to formulate a production plan. However, before it can accurately gauge production needs, it should survey inventory already on hand in order to forecast accurately what must be produced. Delta checks records to see how many units of each of its products it has already on hand. Assume that Delta desires to keep 10 percent of current year's sales on hand to start the next year. Then Delta's production requirements would be calculated, based on inventory on hand:

Cabinets	300
Chairs	400
Desks	200
Benches	2,100

To calculate how much of each item Delta has to produce, add sales requirements and 10 percent inventory required at the end of the period, then subtract inventory already on hand. For instance Delta plans to sell 800 cabinets over the next year. It wants to keep 10 percent on hand to start the year after that, so it would require 880 cabinets; however there already are 300 on hand so Delta needs to produce 580 cabinets over the next year. Calculations for other items are illustrated in Table 3.6.

Obviously poor planning in the past has hurt Delta. Had it planned better in the past its inventory and production would have been in better order. At any

Table 3.2
Monthly Sales Forecasts—Quarter One

January

Cabinets	140 at $200	$28,000
Chairs	260 at 25	6,500
Desks	20 at 150	3,000
Benches	40 at 20	800
TOTAL		$38,300

February

Cabinets	150 at $200	$30,000
Chairs	260 at 25	6,500
Desks	20 at 150	3,000
Benches	40 at 20	800
TOTAL		$40,300

March

Cabinets	150 at $200	$30,000
Chairs	200 at 25	5,000
Desks	20 at 150	3,000
Benches	40 at 20	800
TOTAL		$38,800

Table 3.3
Monthly Sales Forecasts—Quarter Two

April

Cabinets	160 at $200	$32,000
Chairs	200 at 25	5,000
Desks	20 at 150	3,000
Benches	40 at 20	800
TOTAL		$40,800

May

Cabinets	20 at $200	$ 4,000
Chairs	150 at 25	3,750
Desks	20 at 150	3,000
Benches	20 at 20	400
TOTAL		$11,150

June

Cabinets	10 at $200	$ 2,000
Chairs	150 at 25	3,750
Desks	20 at 150	3,000
Benches	20 at 20	400
TOTAL		$ 9,150

Table 3.4
Monthly Sales Forecasts—Quarter Three

July

Cabinets	20 at	$200	$ 4,000
Chairs	150 at	25	3,750
Desks	20 at	150	3,000
Benches	20 at	20	400
TOTAL			$11,150

August

Cabinets	20 at	$200	$ 4,000
Chairs	160 at	25	4,000
Desks	20 at	150	3,000
Benches	20 at	20	400
TOTAL			$11,400

September

Cabinets	40 at	$200	$ 8,000
Chairs	30 at	25	750
Desks	10 at	150	1,500
Benches	40 at	20	800
TOTAL			$11,050

Table 3.5
Monthly Sales Forecasts—Quarter Four

October

Cabinets	40 at	$200	$ 8,000
Chairs	20 at	25	500
Desks	10 at	150	1,500
Benches	40 at	20	800
TOTAL			$10,800

November

Cabinets	40 at	$200	$ 8,000
Chairs	10 at	25	250
Desks	10 at	150	1,500
Benches	80 at	20	1,600
TOTAL			$11,350

December

Cabinets	10 at	$200	$ 2,000
Chairs	10 at	25	250
Desks	10 at	150	1,500
Benches	100 at	20	2,000
TOTAL			$ 5,750

Figure 3.1
Seasonal Sales Fluctuations

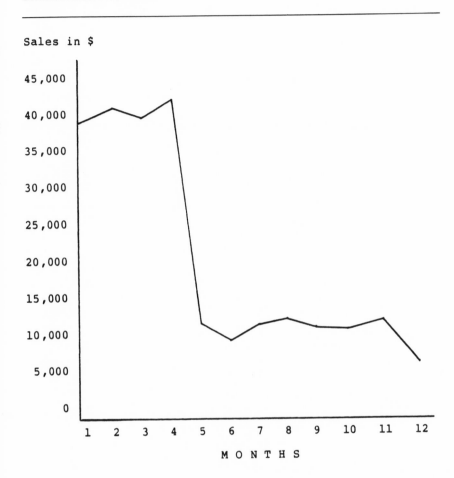

Sales in $

rate, Delta is now ready to begin estimating the costs of next year's inventory. It has $70,000 worth of inventory on the books, calculated in the following fashion:

Cabinets	300 units at $100 cost	$30,000
Chairs	400 units at $10 cost	4,000
Desks	200 units at $75 cost	15,000
Benches	2,100 units at $10 cost	21,000
TOTAL		$70,000

Table 3.6
Production Requirements

Chairs

Sales requirements	1600
10% inventory	160
Already on hand	-400
NEED TO PRODUCE	1360

Desks

Sales requirements	200
10% Inventory	20
Already on hand	-200
NEED TO PRODUCE	20

Benches

Sales requirements	500
10% inventory	50
Already on hand	-2100

NO NEED TO PRODUCE ANY
BENCHES THIS YEAR

The cost for each item was found by adding component labor, material, and overhead costs for producing each of the items. The same procedure should be followed for estimating the value of the ending inventory for next year.

ENDING INVENTORY

The value of Delta's ending inventory would be calculated by estimating component raw materials, labor, and overhead expenses. By assessing past inventory requirements and factoring new cost information such estimates can be achieved:

	Cabinets	Chairs	Desks
Labor	$60.00	$7.00	$55.00
Materials	50.00	5.00	65.00
Overhead	27.50	3.00	22.50
TOTAL	$137.50	$15.00	$142.50

Remember, since Delta already overproduced on benches, it will produce none this year; therefore, cost of benches is still $10 per unit. There will be 1,600 benches in ending inventory (2,100 − 500). Now the value of ending inventory for other products may be calculated by multiplying units of ending inventory by costs per unit:

Cabinets	80 ×	$137.50 =	$11,000
Chairs	160 ×	15.00 =	2,400
Desks	20 ×	142.50 =	2,850
Benches	1,600 ×	10.00 =	16,000
TOTAL			32,250

PRODUCTION PLAN

By assessing current inventory, anticipated sales, and desired ending inventory, a production plan can be formulated. Production is not cut-and-dried; a great deal of planning must go into this stage, examining such issues as labor relations and the health of production equipment.

COST OF GOODS SOLD

The cost of producing the materials for this financial period have already been calculated, but that does not represent the cost of goods sold. Inventory movements of course are responsible for the discrepancy. The costing of goods sold depends upon the particular inventory method used. In this case assume Delta uses FIFO, or first-in first-out inventory. In that case, Delta will sell off all the "old" inventory first, and only when all the old inventory is exhausted will it dip into the "new" inventory. The process of costing Delta's goods sold is illustrated in Table 3.7. The costing based on this information is calculated in Table 3.8.

PRO FORMA INCOME STATEMENT

Now Delta is ready to put together its first version of the pro forma income statement. The "top" part of the statement is already completed—that is, from

Table 3.7
Inventory Movement

Cabinets

    Sales   800

    From Old Inventory   300

    From New Inventory   500

Chairs

    Sales   1,600

    From Old Inventory   400

    From New Inventory   1,200

Desks

    Sales   200

    From Old Inventory   200

    From New Inventory   0

Benches - All from Old

---

sales down to cost of goods sold. Based on trends from the past and projections about costs and the like for the next financial period, the rest of the pro forma income statement might be formulated as in Table 3.9.

CASH BUDGET

The formulation of the cash budget is a multifaceted process. The first step is to analyze past cash inflows and outflows to ascertain probabilistic relationships. Delta has done so, and has determined that past experience shows that it collects 50 percent of all sales in the month they occur, 30 percent within 30 days, and 20 percent within 60 days. A collection schedule for Delta might be drawn.

It is necessary for determination of January collections to know that Delta had sales of $8,200 in November of the previous year, and $4,500 in December. To determine collections for January, for instance, Delta would determine 50 percent of its current sales (50 percent of \$38,300 = \$19,150), add 30 percent of December sales (30 percent of \$4,500 = \$1,350), and 20 percent of November sales (20 percent of \$8,200 = \$1,640) for total collections that month of \$22,140. The following months might be estimated in the same manner as illustrated in Table 3.10.

Assume that, based on past data, Delta projects routine cash outflows for each month as shown in Table 3.11. Assume also that Delta decides to buy another \$12,000 worth of productive equipment. It plans to buy it in January for cash. Assume also that it pays quarterly tax deposits. The tax payments will be made in four installments; and interest charges will be paid every six months. Those adjustments are reflected in Table 3.12.

Table 3.8
Cost of Goods Sold

Cabinets

	From Old	300 x \$100	\$30,000	
	From New	500 x \$137.50	68,750	
	TOTAL COST OF GOODS CABINETS			\$98,750

Chairs

	From Old	400 x \$ 10	4,000	
	From New	1,200 x \$ 15	18,000	
	TOTAL COST OF GOODS CHAIRS			22,000

Desks (all from old)

| | 200 x \$ 75 | | | 15,000 |

Benches (all from old)

| | 500 x \$ 10 | | | 5,000 |

TOTAL COST OF GOODS SOLD - ALL PRODUCTS   \$140,750

Table 3.9
Pro Forma Income Statement, Delta Company

Sales	$240,000
Cost of Goods Sold	140,750
Gross Profits	99,250
Selling & Administrative Costs	27,500
Earnings Before Interest & Taxes	71,750
Interest *	8,400
Earnings Before Taxes	63,350
Taxes **	31,675
NET INCOME	31,675

* Based on last year's interest cost. As Delta goes through the planning process, it may want to adjust this amount, should it decide to seek additional financing or pay off old debt.

** Assuming 50 percent taxes

Table 3.10
Collections

MONTH	SALES	50% CURRENT	30%-30 DAYS	20%-60 DAYS	TOTAL
1	38,300	19,150	1,350	1,640	22,140
2	40,300	20,150	11,490	900	32,540
3	38,800	19,400	12,090	7,660	39,150
4	40,800	20,400	11,640	8,060	40,100
5	11,150	5,575	12,240	7,760	25,575
6	9,150	4,575	3,345	8,160	16,080
7	11,150	5,575	2,745	2,230	10,550
8	11,400	5,700	3,345	1,830	10,875
9	11,050	5,525	3,420	2,230	11,175
10	10,800	5,400	3,315	2,280	10,995
11	11,350	5,675	3,24U	2,210	11,125
12	5,750	2,875	3,405	2,160	8,440

Table 3.11
Routine Cash Outflows

MONTH	CASH OUTFLOWS	MONTH	CASH OUTFLOWS
January	25,000	July	15,000
February	22,000	August	14,000
March	20,000	September	14,000
April	28,000	October	12,000
May	15,000	November	12,000
June	15,000	December	12,000

Table 3.12
Cash Outflows—Total

MONTH	ROUTINE CASH OUTFLOWS	FIXED ASSETS	TAX DEPOSITS	INTEREST PMTS.	TOTAL
January	25,000	12,000			37,000
February	22,000				22,000
March	20,000		7,919		27,919
April	28,000				28,000
May	15,000				15,000
June	15,000		7,919	4,200	27,119
July	15,000				15,000
August	14,000				14,000
September	14,000		7,919		21,919
October	12,000				12,000
November	12,000				12,000
December	12,000		7,919*	4,200**	24,119

 *one-fourth of estimated taxes
**one-half of estimated interest expenses

Assume that Delta starts the year with $20,000 in cash and it desires a monthly minimum balance of $5,000. If it doesn't have enough to keep $5,000 minimum, it borrows on a line of credit with the bank. If there is anything outstanding on its line of credit and if there is a surplus in any month, then Delta will pay down on the outstanding loan balance. The results will look something like those shown in Table 3.13.

PRO FORMA BALANCE SHEET

Once management has completed all the previous steps, then the pro forma balance sheet can be pieced together. Each of the items in Delta's beginning balance sheet is presented in Table 3.14. Then an explanation of how each amount in the pro forma statement was formulated is presented in Table 3.15.

Table 3.13
Cash Flows and Loan Balances

MONTH	BEG. CASH BALANCE	CASH INFLOWS	CASH OUTFLOWS	SURPLUS (DEFICIT)	LOAN BALANCE
January	20,000	22,140	37,000	5,140	
February	5,140	32,540	22,000	15,680	
March	15,680	39,150	27,919	26,911	
April	26,911	40,100	28,000	39,011	
May	39,011	25,575	15,000	49,586	
June	49,586	16,080	27,119	38,547	
July	38,547	10,550	15,000	34,097	
August	34,097	10,875	14,000	30,972	
September	30,972	11,175	21,919	20,228	
October	20,228	10,995	12,000	19,223	
November	19,223	11,125	12,000	18,348	
December	18,348	8,440	24,119	2,669	2,331*

*Delta wanted a $5,000 minimum balance, so they had to borrow $2,331 ($5,000 − $2,669)

Table 3.14
Delta Company 19X1 Balance Sheet

Cash	$20,000	Accounts Payable	$ 10,000
Mkt. Sec	10,000	Accruals	4,000
Receivables	50,000	Notes Payable	24,000
Inventory	70,000		
Fixed Assets	160,000	Long-Term Debt	96,000
		Common Stock	64,000
		Retained Earnings	112,000
TOTAL	310,000	TOTAL	310,000

Table 3.15
Calculation of New Balance Sheet Items

ITEM	AMOUNT	HOW DERIVED
Cash	$ 5,000	From cash budget - balance in December
Mkt Sec.	10,000	From beginning balance sheet – management may decide to sell or increase or simply leave the same
Rec.	5,145	From collections information. 50% of December's sales ($2,875) plus 20% of November's ($2,270) was left to be collected. $2,875 + $2,270 = $5,145.
Inv.	32,250	Value of ending inventory
Fixed Assets	172,000	Last year's balance plus new assets of $12,000
Total Assets	224,395	Total of all of above
Total Claims	224,395	Must equal total assets
Acc. Pay	10,000	In this case, Delta figured based on last year's expenditures. Will vary depending on production needs and payables strategy
Accruals	4,000	Again, depends on production plans
Common Stock	64,000	Same as last year
Ret. Earn.	143,675	Last year's retained earnings balance, $112,000 + this year's addition to retained earnings from pro forma income statement, $31,675

Right now if we subtract all Delta's claims from total assets, there is only $2,720 left: $224,395 − 10,000 − 4,000 − 64,000 − 143,675 = $2,720. That means that if Delta's plans for the coming year work out, some resources are freed up. Delta would be able to pay off all but $22,670 of old debt, or it might decide to pay out some of the retained earnings in the form of dividends. This outcome would be a boon to Delta. Oftentimes, however, during the planning process the opposite circumstances occur. It is likely that a company finds during its projections that in order to support the asset base required by additional sales it needs additional financing. This might be called an external funds requirement. An example of dealing with an external funds requirement is covered in Chapter 4.

In this case, though, Delta has the welcome task of deciding what to do with the extra resources to be created over the next year. Whatever it decides will of course impact on some of the statements that have already been prepared, such as the pro forma income statement and the cash budget. When Delta decides what strategy or strategies it wants to follow, it will have to adjust these statements.

Assume that Delta just decided to pay off all debt it could, starting with short-term notes payable. Then its pro forma balance sheet would look like that in Table 3.16. Now, of course, when the resulting statements are perused, other questions might arise. Resulting strategies might be analyzed and all the statements might be redrawn. For example, Delta might worry that based on pro forma projections, it doesn't like what it sees and wants to revise its plans. Again any changes will necessitate redoing pro forma statements.

For example, assume that Delta decides that if it proceeded as planned, its shareholders will not be happy with the results. Therefore, it goes back into consultation. It decides that by redoing its ad campaign and revamping sales

Table 3.16
Delta Company 19X2 Balance Sheet

Cash	$ 5,000	Accounts Payable	$ 10,000
Mkt. Sec	10,000	Accruals	4,000
Receivbls.	5,145	Notes Payable	-0-
Inventory	32,250		
Fixed Assets	172,000	Long-Term Debt	2,720
		Common Stock	64,000
		Retained Earnings	143,675
TOTAL	224,395	TOTAL	224,395

training and sales motivation (at no extra expense), it could add another 8 percent
to the sales forecast. In consulting with the credit and collections managers, it
is decided that collections could be accelerated. Now Delta predicts that it can
collect 55 percent of all sales in the month they occur, 40 percent within 30
days, and 5 percent within 60 days. Delta will still buy the $12,000 worth of
productive equipment needed. The purchase will be made in January and paid
for in February. Assume also that labor costs went down 10 percent. Resulting
changes are shown in Tables 3.17–3.36.

Table 3.17
Sales Forecast—Annual

Cabinets	864 at $200		$172,800
Chairs	1728 at 25		43,200
Desks	216 at 150		32,400
Benches	540 at 20		10,800*
TOTAL SALES FOR YEAR			*260,025 (Actual); Rounding error

Table 3.18
Monthly Sales Forecast—Quarter One

January			
Cabinets	151 at $200		$30,200
Chairs	281 at 25		7,025
Desks	22 at 150		3,300
Benches	43 at 20		860
TOTAL			$41,385
February			
Cabinets	162 at $200		$32,400
Chairs	281 at 25		7,025
Desks	22 at 150		3,300
Benches	43 at 20		860
TOTAL			$43,585

Table 3.18 (cont.)

```
    March

            Cabinets        162 at $200              $32,400

            Chairs          216 at    25               5,400

            Desks            22 at   150               3,300

            Benches          43 at    20                 860

            TOTAL                                     $41,960
```

Table 3.19
Monthly Sales Forecast—Quarter Two

```
    April

            Cabinets        173 at $200              $34,600

            Chairs          216 at    25               5,400

            Desks            22 at   150               3,300

            Benches          43 at    20                 860

            TOTAL                                     $44,160

    May

            Cabinets         22 at $200              $ 4,400

            Chairs          162 at    25               4,050

            Desks            22 at   150               3,300

            Benches          22 at    20                 440

            TOTAL                                     $12,190

    June

            Cabinets         11 at $200              $ 2,200

            Chairs          162 at    25               4,050

            Desks            22 at   150               3,300

            Benches          22 at    20                 440

            TOTAL                                       9,990
```

Table 3.20
Monthly Sales Forecast—Quarter Three

July

Cabinets	22 at $200	$ 4,400
Chairs	162 at 25	4,050
Desks	22 at 150	3,300
Benches	22 at 20	440
TOTAL		$12,190

August

Cabinets	22 at $200	$ 4,400
Chairs	173 at 25	4,325
Desks	22 at 150	3,300
Benches	22 at 20	440
TOTAL		$12,465

September

Cabinets	43 at $200	$ 8,600
Chairs	32 at 25	800
Desks	11 at 150	1,650
Benches	43 at 20	860
TOTAL		$11,910

Table 3.21
Monthly Sales Forecast—Quarter Four

October

Cabinets	43 at $200	$ 8,600
Chairs	22 at 25	550
Desks	11 at 150	1,650
Benches	43 at 20	860
TOTAL		$11,660

Table 3.21 (cont.)

November

Cabinets	43 at $200	$ 8,600
Chairs	11 at 25	275
Desks	11 at 150	1,650
Benches	86 at 20	1,720
TOTAL		$12,245

December

Cabinets	11 at $200	$ 2,200
Chairs	11 at 25	275
Desks	11 at 150	1,650
Benches	108 at 20	2,160
TOTAL		$ 6,285

Table 3.22
Production Requirements

Chairs

Sales requirements	1729
10% inventory	173
Already on hand	- 400
NEED TO PRODUCE	1502

Desks

Sales requirements	220
10% inventory	22
Already on hand	- 200
NEED TO PRODUCE	42

Table 3.22 (cont.)

```
Cabinets
        Sales requirements                    864
        10% inventory                          86
        Already on Hand                     - 300
        NEED TO PRODUCE                       650
Benches
        Sales requirements                    540
        10% inventory                          54
        Already on hand                     -2100
        NO NEED TO PRODUCE ANY BENCHES THIS YEAR
```

Table 3.23
Inventory on Hand

```
                Cabinets         300
                Chairs           400
                Desks            200
                Benches          2100
```

Table 3.24
Value of Beginning Inventory

```
        Cabinets        300 units at $100 cost        $30,000
        Chairs          400 units at $10 cost           4,000
        Desks           200 units at $75 cost          15,000
        Benches         2100 units at $10 cost         21,000
        TOTAL                                         $70,000
```

Table 3.25
Inventory Costing

	Cabinets	Chairs	Desks
Labor	54.00	6.30	49.50
Materials	50.00	5.00	65.00
Overhead	27.50	3.00	22.50
TOTAL	131.50	14.30	137.00

Table 3.26
Value of Ending Inventory

Cabinets	87	x	131.50	=	$11,440.50
Chairs	173	x	14.30	=	2,473.90
Desks	22	x	137.00	=	3,014.00
Benches	1,060	x	10.00	=	10,600.00
TOTAL					$27,528.40

Table 3.27
Inventory Movement

Cabinets	
Sales	865
From Old Inventory	300
From New Inventory	565
Chairs	
Sales	1,729
From Old Inventory	400
From New Inventory	1,329
Desks	
Sales	220
From Old Inventory	200
From New Inventory	20
Benches	
All from Old	

Table 3.28
Cost of Goods Sold

Cabinets				
From Old	300	x	100.00	$ 30,000.00
From New	565	x	131.50	74,297.50
TOTAL COST OF GOODS CABINETS				$104,297.50
Chairs				
From Old	400	x	10.00	4,000.00
From New	1329	x	14.30	19,004.70
TOTAL COST OF GOODS CHAIRS				$ 23,004.70
Desks				
From Old	200	x	75.00	15,000.00
From New	20	x	137.00	2,740.00
TOTAL COST OF GOODS DESKS				$ 17,740.00
Benches				
From Old	540	x	10.00	5,400.00
TOTAL COSTS OF GOODS SOLD - ALL PRODUCTS				$150,442.20

Table 3.29
Pro Forma Income Statement—Delta Company

Sales	$260,025.00
Cost of Goods Sold	150,442.20
Gross Profits	109,582.80
Selling and Administrative Costs	29,902.88
Earnings Before Interest and Taxes	79,679.92
Interest *	8,400.00
Earnings Before Taxes	71,279.92
Taxes **	35,639.96
NET INCOME	34,639.96

* Based on last year's interest cost. As Delta goes through the planning process, it may want to adjust this amount, should it decide to seek additional financing or pay off old debt.

** Assuming 50 percent taxes.

Table 3.30
Collections

Month	Sales	55% Current	40%-30 Days	5%-60 Days	Total
1	41,385	22,761.75	* 1,350	**1,640.00	25,751.75
2	43,585	23,971.75	16,554	** 900.00	41,425.75
3	41,960	23,078.00	17,434	2,069.25	42,581.25
4	44,160	24,288.00	16,784	2,179.25	43,251.25
5	12,190	6,704.50	17,664	2,098.00	26,466.50
6	9,990	5,494.50	4,876	2,208.00	12,578.50
7	12,190	6,704.50	3,996	609.50	11,310.00
8	12,465	6,855.75	4,876	499.50	12,231.25
9	11,910	6,550.50	4,986	609.50	12,146.00
10	11,660	6,413.00	4,764	623.25	11,800.25
11	12,245	6,734.75	4,664	595.50	11,994.25
12	6,285	3,456.75	4,898	583.00	8,937.75

* Based on last years 30% - 30 Days collection

** Based on last years 20% - 60 Days collection

Table 3.31
Routine Cash Outflows

MONTH	CASH OUTFLOWS*	MONTH	CASH OUTFLOWS*
January	25,000	July	15,000
February	22,000	August	14,000
March	20,000	September	14,000
April	28,000	October	12,000
May	15,000	November	12,000
June	15,000	December	12,000

* Do not reflect any changes for change
  in purchase due to production changes.
  May want to adjust for such changes.

Table 3.32
Cash Outflows—Total

MONTH	ROUTINE CASH OUTFLOWS	FIXED ASSETS	TAX DEPOSITS	INTEREST PMTS.	TOTAL
January	25,000	0			25,000
February	22,000	12,000			34,000
March	20,000		8,909.99		28,909.99
April	28,000				28,000
May	15,000				15,000
June	15,000		8,909.99	4,200**	28,109.99
July	15,000				15,000
August	14,000				14,000
September	14,000		8,909.99		22,909.99
October	12,000				12,000
November	12,000				12,000
December	12,000		8,909.99	4,200	25,109.99

* one-fourth of estimated taxes

** one-half of estimated interest expenses

Table 3.33
Cash Flows

Month	Beg. Cash Balance	Cash Inflows	Cash Outflows	Surplus (Deficit)	Loan Balance
January	5,000.00	25,751.75	25,000.00	5,751.75	0
February	5,751.75	41,425.75	34,000.00	13,177.50	0
March	13,177.50	42,581.25	28,909.99	26,848.76	0
April	26,848.76	43,251.25	28,000.00	42,100.01	0
May	42,100.01	26,466.50	15,000.00	53,566.51	0
June	53,566.51	12,578.50	28,109.99	38,035.02	0
July	38,035.02	11,310.00	15,000.00	34,345.02	0
August	34,345.02	12,231.25	14,000.00	32,576.27	0
September	32,576.27	12,146.00	22,909.99	21,812.28	0
October	21,812.28	11,800.25	12,000.00	21,612.53	0
November	21,612.53	11,994.25	12,000.00	21,606.78	0
December	21,606.78	8,937.75	25,109.99	5,434.54	0

Table 3.34
Delta Company 19X1 Balance Sheet

Cash	$ 20,000	Accounts Payable	$ 10,000
Mkt. Sec.	10,000	Accruals	4,000
Receivables	50,000	Notes Payable	24,000
Inventory	70,000		
Fixed Assets	160,000	Long-Term Debt	96,000
		Common Stock	64,000
		Retained Earnings	112,000
TOTAL	310,000	TOTAL	310,000

Table 3.35
Calculation of New Balance Sheet Items

ITEM	AMOUNT	HOW DERIVED
Cash	$ 5,435.54	From cash budget - balance in December
Mkt. Sec.	10,000.00	From beginning balance sheet - management may decide to sell or simply leave the same
Rec.	3,440.50	From collections information. $2,828.25 from December sales + 612.25 from November sales
Inv.	27,528.40	From Table 3.26. Value of ending inventory
Fixed Assets	172,000.00	Last year's balance plus new assets of $12,000
Total Assets	218,403.44	Total of all of above
Total Claims	218,403.44	Must equal total assets
Common Stock	64,000.00	Same as last year
Ret. Earn.	147,639.96	Last year's retained earnings balance, $112,000 + this year's addition to retained earnings - $35,639.96
Other Claims	6,763.48	$218,403.44 - $147,639.96 - $64,000 = $6,763.48

Delta can pay off all old debts but $6,763.48
Assume Delta pays off all but $6,763.48 long-term debt

Table 3.36
Delta Company 19X2 Pro Forma Balance Sheet

Cash	$ 5,434.54	Long-Term Debt	$ 6,763.48
Mkt. Sec.	10,000.00	Common Stock	64,000.00
Rec.	3,440.50	Ret. Earnings	147,639.96
Inventory	27,528.40		
Fixed Assets	172,000.00		
TOTAL	$218,403.44	TOTAL	$218,403.44

_____ 4 _____

THE BASIC SHORTCUT
FORECASTING MODEL

Chapter 3 illustrated all the steps in a full-blown planning process. It also conveyed a sense of the importance of the process. Throughout all the steps in the process, questions are asked and answered. A plan of action for the company develops. At times, however, a shortcut to this process might be appropriate. If a company is "trying on" different financial strategies or the like, a quick look at the bottom line is appropriate. In that case, strategists would not want to expend energy going through all the statements and such outlined in Chapter 3; they would want to look quickly at a pro forma income statement and balance sheet to gauge roughly the impact of any strategies. In that case, a shortcut technique is extremely helpful.

A shortcut method should not be used in exclusion of the full-blown planning process, however. Shortcuts don't allow all aspects of the planning process to be examined, nor do they force a strategist into asking all the questions necessary to good planning. Therefore, shortcuts should never be used as a substitute for full-blown planning, but rather as a supplement.

A basic shortcut forecasting model is presented in this chapter. This model is often called the percent of sales method, which is developed from the idea that a company's assets, liabilities, and expenses are related to the company's sales volume. Generally speaking, the larger a company's sales are, the larger its other accounts might be. It should already be apparent that a good sales forecast is important. Using the tools covered in Chapter 3, you should be able to prepare a good sales forecast. This chapter assumes that a sales forecast has already been made; now the pro forma financial statements will be prepared from the forecast of sales. The first section of this chapter covers pro forma balance sheets. The second covers pro forma income statements. The next section illustrates the reconciliation of the pro forma income statement with the pro forma balance sheet. This reconciliation is necessary because the two financial statements are interrelated.

FORECASTING THE BALANCE SHEET

Most balance sheet accounts are closely related to changes in sales. This is an important point that must be understood. Inventory is an excellent example. If a company wants to increase its sales (assuming that the management is not trying to change the inventory management system at the same time), inventory has to increase to accommodate the larger sales volume. The more the company sells, the more raw materials it will have to keep on hand, the more work-in-process generated, and the more finished goods it will have to keep on hand in order to meet anticipated sales increases. Accounts receivable is another good example. The more a company sells, the more customers will charge on account, and the more accounts receivable will increase.

While the relationship between other balance sheet accounts and sales may not be so obvious, the relationships do exist. When an account is directly related to sales, the account is called *spontaneous*. A spontaneous asset is one that increases (spontaneously) when sales increase. A spontaneous liability is one that increases when sales increase. Certainly, management can prevent a spontaneous account from increasing, and in some instances may want to do just that. However, in the absence of specific management action preventing the spontaneous increase, a spontaneous account will rise when sales rise. Generally, cash, accounts receivable, and inventory are considered to be spontaneous assets. These accounts are positively related to sales.

Marketable securities are not related to sales. Instead, marketable securities are changed when management makes a decision to invest excess cash or to sell off existing securities. These accounts change only when a specific management decision is made to change these accounts. Therefore, marketable securities and similar accounts are considered nonspontaneous.

Fixed assets are *quasi-spontaneous*. It would be inaccurate to believe that fixed assets increase when sales increase. However, if a company has reached its practical fixed asset capacity, to increase sales will require an increase in the fixed asset. Fixed asset expenditures generally are made in large lump-sum purchases. For example, if sales are expected to increase a little each year over the next ten years, it would not be in a company's best interests to build ten small factories during each of the next ten years. More often than not, it is less expensive to plan ahead and build a factory to handle the growth of several years.

Some liabilities may also be considered spontaneous. For example, accounts payable, taxes payable, and accruals generally are related to sales volume. As sales increase, a company must make more expenditures, so its accounts payables and accruals will rise. If its new sales are profitable, taxes payable will rise too.

Once again, management could prevent the increases from happening, but unless they prevent it, the increases will occur. Liabilities that require specific negotiation with a lender are not considered to be spontaneous.

Notes payables, bank loans, and bonds are not spontaneous. While they may increase from time to time, when they do so it is the result of a management decision. The increases are not spontaneous. Equity accounts are not spontaneous. To increase common or preferred stock requires specific management action. Management may decide to increase one of these accounts in response to sales increases, but such action does not occur spontaneously.

Retained earnings is different from other equity accounts. Retained earnings is a quasi-spontaneous account. If a company's sales increase, retained earnings will increase only if the new sales are profitable and only if the dividend payout ratio is not increased to offset the increased profitability. To find out how much retained earnings will increase, add the new retained earnings to the previous balance. The new retained earnings will be the expected total sales multiplied by the company's profit margin (ratio of net income to sales), which is multiplied by the company's retention ratio (one minus the payout ratio). This computation is a simplification. It presumes that profits increase at the same rate as the company's sales. This issue is covered more completely when the income statement and the balance sheet are reconciled in the next section. An example of pro forma balance sheet preparation follows.

Example

The 19X1 balance sheet for the Delta Company appears in Table 4.1. Delta is a producer of fine furniture. There is nothing outstanding to note about this balance sheet; however, the spontaneous accounts, cash, receivables, inventory, accounts payable, and accruals are readily identified. The Delta Company is operating at its fixed asset capacity, so any sales increases will require new fixed assets. Its profit margin is 5 percent and Delta keeps a 40 percent payout ratio.

The management of Delta Company is expecting a sales increase of 20 percent in 19X2. This estimate is based upon a thorough market analysis prepared by an outside marketing analysis and consulting firm. Since fixed assets are at their practical capacity, new fixed assets costing $24,000 must be purchased. In addition, the current notes payable are due and must be paid off during the year. In Table 4.2 a pro forma balance sheet has been prepared based upon the facts outlined above. It is helpful to examine each account to determine how the balance was computed.

Cash is the first account listed, and it is a spontaneous asset. Since sales will increase by 20 percent, the model assumes that cash will increase by 20 percent as well. The predicted cash balance is $24,000, a 20 percent increase over the 19X1 $20,000 balance. Management may not want an increase in cash of 20 percent and can certainly prevent it. However, in the absence of specific management action, the increase will occur. Management control of these sponta-

Table 4.1
Delta Company 19X1 Balance Sheet

Cash	$ 20,000	Accounts Payable	$ 10,000
Marketable Securitites	10,000	Accruals	4,000
Receivables	50,000	Notes Payable @ 10%	24,000
Inventory	70,000	Total	$ 38,000
Total	$150,000	Long-term Debt @ 15%	96,000
Net Fixed Assets	160,000	Common Stock	64,000
		Retained Earnings	112,000
Total Assets	$310,000	Total	$310,000

Other Selected Data:

Sales	$200,000
Net Income	10,000
Dividends	4,000

Table 4.2
19X2 Pro Forma Balance Sheet

Cash (20,000 X 1.2)	$ 24,000	Accounts Payable (10,000 X 1.2)	$ 12,000
Marketable Securities	10,000	Accruals (4,000 X 1.2)	4,800
Receivables (50,000 X 1.2)	60,000	Notes Payable (paid off)	-0-
Inventory (70,000 X 1.2)	84,000	Total	$ 16,800
Total	$178,000	Long-Term Debt (same)	96,000
		Common Stock (same)	64,000
Net Fixed Assets (160,000 + 24,000)	184,000	Retained Earnings*	119,200
		Subtotal	296,000
		EFR	66,000
Total Assets	362,000	Total	362,000

$$*112{,}000 + (240{,}000)\left(\frac{10{,}000}{200{,}000}\right)\left(1 - \frac{4000}{10{,}000}\right) = \underline{119{,}200}$$

NOTES: 1. 20% sales increase in 19X2
2. Fixed asset increase of $24,000 will be required
3. The current notes payable are due

neous accounts is discussed in more depth in Chapters 5–7. One final point must be made at this time. The relationship between cash and sales may be a more complicated relationship than that expressed by a simple percentage. This will be explored more thoroughly in Chapter 8.

Marketable securities is the next account listed. A comparison of Tables 4.1 and 4.2 reveals that the balance remained the same. Marketable securities is not spontaneous. Unless Delta's management decides to adjust this balance, it will remain the same. Receivables and Inventory are considered spontaneous. Their pro forma balances increase by 20 percent over the balance in 19X1.

Fixed assets increase by a net amount of $24,000. Fixed assets are not related to sales in the same way as the truly spontaneous accounts. Instead, Delta's management obtained estimates for the needed fixed assets and decided to make the purchase. The $24,000 is added to the previous period's balance.

The total assets are $362,000. The liabilities and equities must total to this amount also. Accounts payable and accruals are spontaneous. Their balance is expected to increase by 20 percent over the 19X1 balance. The notes payable are due in 19X2. Unless management decides to renew them, this balance will drop to zero as shown in Table 4.2.

Long-term debt and common stock will not change, at least not at this stage of the planning process. Their balances remain constant. The pro forma retained earnings balance is $119,200. This balance is arrived at in the computation at the bottom of Table 4.2. The 19X1 retained earning's balance, $112,000, is increased by the new retained earnings. The new retained earnings is found by multiplying the total expected 19X2 sales, $240,000, by the profit margin, $10,000/$200,000, and by the retention ratio, $1 - (\$4,000/\$10,000)$. The product of the first two terms, sales times the profit margin, provides a rough estimate for the 19X2 profit.

The profit estimate times the retention ratio provides the expected increase in retained earnings. Summing the liabilities and equities shows a balance of $296,000, which is $66,000 short of the asset balance. The total increase in the assets was greater than the increase in the liabilities and equities. 38 This $66,000 difference might be called the External Financing Requirement (EFR). The EFR shows how much Delta will have to raise in order to support the new asset base it projects. The EFR exists because when a company's sales grow, generally the accompanying growth in assets is not offset by spontaneous growth in liabilities and equities. It is ironic that a company that is extremely profitable and is growing very fast will have to raise considerably more external funds than a static company.

At this stage of the forecasting procedure, Delta management must decide how to raise the EFR. New long-term debt or a common stock sale may be used. Most corporate finance books discuss capital structure and financing decisions if one wishes to examine this issue in more depth. However, this decision is beyond the scope of this book. This example deals only with the forecast after this decision has been made. One final way to deal with the EFR is to reduce the growth in the assets. Perhaps better asset management would reduce the external funding requirements. Planning for growth is an important aspect of management, and growth considerations are covered in Chapters 6 and 7.

Suppose that management decided to raise the $66,000 with a common stock sale. The only change to the balance sheet in Table 4.2 would be the common stock account. Its balance would rise to $130,000, an amount that is $66,000 larger than its present balance. At this juncture, the balance sheet is put aside for a moment. We will return to it in a following section to combine it with the income statement. In the next section, the forecasted income statement will be examined. The same percent of sales model will be used.

THE FORECASTED INCOME STATEMENT

In the previous section, a simplification—that net income would remain a fixed percentage of sales—was used to find net income. The profit margin was used to convert the sales estimate to the net income estimate. In this section a pro forma income statement is constructed. The percent of sales method will be used in this section as well.

An income statement will include estimates for sales and for various expenses. Most expenses will be related to sales. As sales go up, expenses will rise as well. In this chapter, however, no distinction is made between fixed and variable costs. In later chapters adjustments will be illustrated. To construct the income statement from the percent of sales method, each item on the most recent income statement must be computed as a percent of sales. These percentages are then applied to the sales estimate to obtain the estimated balances in these accounts. An example is the best way to learn the procedure.

Example

The 19X1 Delta Company income statement appears in Table 4.3. The income is $10,000 from sales of $200,000. The interest expense is based upon the 10 percent notes payable and the 15 percent long-term debt. Interest computation is included at the bottom of the income statement. Delta is still expecting a 20 percent sales increase in 19X2 over the 19X1 sales. In Table 4.4 the 19X2 pro forma income statement is presented. In Table 4.3 the cost of goods sold was 55 percent of sales. This percentage is applied to the estimated sales. Cost of goods sold is estimated to be $132,000 in 19X2. This leaves Delta with gross profits amounting to $108,000. Selling and administrative expenses were 26.6 percent of sales in 19X1. Applying this percentage to the 19X2 sales estimate produces selling and administrative expenses of $63,840. Subtracting this expense from gross profit gives the earnings before interest and taxes, EBIT, of $44,160. EBIT is 18.4 percent of sales in 19X1 and in the 19X2 estimate.

Table 4.3
Delta Company 19X1 Income Statement

	$	%
Sales	200,000	100.0
Cost of Goods Sold	-110,000	- 55.0
Gross Profit	90,000	45.0
Selling and Admin. Expenses	- 53,200	- 26.6
EBIT	36,800	18.4
Interest*	- 16,800	- 8.4
EBT	20,000	10.0
Taxes (50%)	- 10,000	- 5.0
Net Income	10,000	5.0

```
*Notes Payable    24,000 @ 10% =   2,400
 Long-Term Debt   96,000 @ 15% =  14,400
        Total Interest           16,800
```

Table 4.4
Delta Company 19X2 Pro Forma Income Statement

	$	%
Sales	240,000	100.0
Cost of Goods Sold	-132,000	-55.0
Gross Profit	108,000	45.0
Selling and Admin. Expenses	- 63,840	-26.6
EBIT	44,160	18.4
Interest*	- 14,400	- 6.0
EBT	29,760	12.4
Taxes (50%)	- 14,880	- 6.2
Net Income**	14,880	6.2

*Assumes that the notes payable are paid off early in 19X2.

**Net Income is not the same percent of sales as Table 4.3, because debt did not remain the same percent of sales.

So far a straight percentage was applied to each of the items in the income statement. However, in the computation of the interest expense, an inconsistency arises: In the balance sheet computation, short-term notes payable were due in 19X2. Therefore, the 19X2 interest expense, in the absence of using debt to finance the EFR, will be $14,400. In other words, from this point on, the income statement can no longer follow the same percentages as 19X1.

Notice that the percent of sales is now 6 percent instead of the 8.4 percent incurred in 19X1. The difference occurred for two reasons. First of all, the notes payable were due in 19X2. Therefore, no interest was paid on them. Second, the strict percent of sales was violated. Interest expense was kept at a particular balance instead of as a percent of sales. In other words, it was treated as a nonspontaneous account. The taxes are assumed to be 50 percent of the earnings before taxes, leaving net income of $14,880. This net income is not the same percentage of sales as the 19X1 income.

Several problems must now be addressed. They will be discussed here but will be solved in the next section. The first problem is that the net income that was found in the income statement was $14,880. The net income that was used in the retained earnings computation in the balance sheet was 5 percent of $240,000, or $12,000. The difference happened because interest expense was treated as a nonspontaneous account. In other words, it was not held to 8.4 percent of sales.

This difference can be reconciled:

$$(8.4\% - 6.0\%) \times \$240,000 \times 50\% = \$2,880$$

Interest expense was 8.4 percent in 19X1 and is expected to be 6.0 percent in 19X2. Multiplying this difference by the $240,000 expected sales and then by the tax rate, 50 percent, produces $2,880. This number is the difference between the interest expense for the two years. Clearly, interest expense will not be 8.4 percent of sales, so the income statement will be the most correct estimate of income. This means that the balance sheet must be adjusted for this new set of information. This correction is made in the next section.

The second problem is the EFR. If the EFR or a portion of the EFR is financed with debt, then a new computation for interest expense is necessary. This fact would render both the income statement and the balance sheet incorrect. As a matter of fact, it makes the computation more difficult because the complete balance sheet is necessary to compute the EFR and the interest computation on the income statement, and the income statement is necessary to complete the retained earnings section on the balance sheet. It is a circular problem. The income statement is needed to find the balance sheet, but the balance sheet is needed to find the income statement. Fortunately, it is not an unsolvable problem. In the next section, this problem and the previous one will be solved.

RECONCILING THE TWO PRO FORMA FINANCIAL STATEMENTS

The two problems that must be solved both deal with the interest computation, and both can be solved in one step. The solution requires an equation with an algebraic manipulation. The procedures for reconciling the income statement and balance sheet are as follows:

1. Prepare a pro forma estimate of the assets and total liabilities. Use the percent of sales method illustrated in the first section of this chapter. Do not prepare an estimate for the retained earnings or the EFR; this will come later.

2. Prepare a pro forma estimate of EBIT. Use the percent of sales method. Remember that the problems with the income statement occur after EBIT, so there is no problem with its preparation.

3. Use this equation to solve for the EFR:
   Old Retained Earnings + (EBIT − Old Interest − New Interest) × (1 − T) (1 − PO) + Total Debt and Common Stock = Pro Forma Assets

This equation is not as overwhelming as it may seem at first glance. The term in the parentheses is the new retained earnings. Notice that it is the bottom section of an income statement in equation form. Both old and new interest expenses are subtracted from EBIT. The new interest is the EFR times the interest rate on the new debt. This gives earnings before interest and taxes. When EBIT is multiplied by one minus the tax rate, T, then the net income is computed. It is based upon the amount of EFR. Multiplying the net income by one minus the payout ratio, PO, gives the incremental addition to retained earnings.

This is added to the existing retained earnings balance to arrive at the pro forma retained earnings balance. The only unknown is the EFR, and it will be found momentarily. The pro forma retained earnings balance is added to the total debt and common stock. Total debt includes any existing debt that will remain on the balance sheet plus any new debt, which is the EFR.

The sum of all of these terms is the total right-hand side of a balance sheet. The total of these liabilities and equities must be equal to the total of the assets. Total pro forma assets are already known, so the next step is to set the liabilities and equities equal to that number. Once again, the easiest way to learn this procedure is with an example.

Example

This example recomputes the income statement and balance sheet for Delta Company for 19X2 using the reconciliation procedure outlined above. The first step in the procedure is to find the pro forma assets. In referring to Table 4.2, the assets total $362,000. The current liabilities can also be found, and they match the total in Table 4.2, $16,800. The existing long-term debt is $96,000 and the common stock is $64,000. The total of all the liabilities and common stock is $176,800. At this point it is necessary to focus attention on the income statement.

The pro forma income statement shown in Table 4.4, is used to find the EBIT, which is $44,160, using the percent of sales method. The tax rate is still 50 percent, and the payout ratio is still 40 percent. Assume that the company will finance the EFR with a long-term debt issue at an effective interest rate equal to 15 percent. Everything necessary to prepare the pro forma financial statement is now known.

In Table 4.5 the reconciliation computation appears. The old retained earnings balance is $112,000. Accounts payable, accruals, old long-term debt, and common stock total $176,800 plus the EFR. This is the old debt, common stock, and new debt (EFR). The incremental retained earnings computation is inside of the brackets. EBIT is $44,160. From EBIT the interest on the existing debt, $14,400, is subtracted. The interest on the new debt must also be subtracted. The new debt is EFR and its interest rate is 15 percent. Therefore, the interest cost on the new debt is (EFR) × (15%).

Income before taxes is multiplied by one minus the tax rate (1 − 50%), and by one minus the payout ratio (1 − 40%). The term in brackets is the new retained earnings. The expression on the left-hand side of the equation is the total new liabilities and equities. It must equal the total of the pro forma assets, $362,000, found above. The equation now has one unknown, EFR. Solving algebraically for EFR produces an amount equal to $67,300. The final version of the pro forma financial statements can now be prepared.

Table 4.5
Reconciliation of the Income Statement and the Balance Sheet

```
Assets = $362,000

Liabilities = Accounts Payable             ($12,000)
              Accruals                      ($ 4,800)
              Old Long-Term Debt            ($96,000)
              Common Stock                  ($64,000)
              Old Retained Earnings        ($112,000)
              EFR                           (   ?   )
              + New Retained Earnings       (   ?   )

New Retained Earnings = EBIT ($44,160) - Interest On Old Debt
     ($14,400) - Interest On New Debt (15% Of EFR) - Taxes (1-.50)
                - Dividends (1-.40)

   362,000 = 12,000 + 4,800 + 96,000 + 64,000 + EFR + 112,000 +
             {[44,160 - 14,400 - (EFR) (.15)] [(1-.50) (1-.40)]}

                         EFR = $67,300
```

In Table 4.6 the reconciled income statement has been prepared. It is the same as before down to EBIT. The new interest computation is based on the existing long-term debt plus the EFR.

In Table 4.7 the reconciled balance sheet appears. The asset side is the same as before. The only difference is in the computation of the retained earnings. The new retained earnings balance is $117,900. It was computed at the bottom of the income statement in Table 4.6. Notice that the EFR is shown as long-term debt, since that was the method of financing. A couple of additional points must be made. The first should be obvious: The balance sheet and income statements prepared in earlier sections are not the correct procedure. The reconciliation is necessary to be entirely accurate. However, the unreconciled statements may be used if a "quick and dirty" estimate is all that is required.

The final point to be made is that debt financing is not the only alternative. Suppose, first of all, that the EFR would come strictly from equity financing. In the reconciliation the (EFR) × (15%) computation would not be made. The

Table 4.6
Delta Company Reconciled Income Statement

Sales	240,000
Cost of Goods Sold	-132,000
Gross Profit	108,000
Selling and Admin. Expenses	- 63,840
EBIT	44,160
Interest*	- 24,495
EBT	19,665
Taxes (50%)	- 9,833
Net Income	9,832
Dividends (40%)	- 3,932
Addition to Retained Earnings	5,900
Beginning Retained Earnings	112,000
Ending Retained Earnings	117,900

*(96,000 + 67,300) (15%) = $24,495

EFR would still be added to long-term debt and common stock, but now it would be considered a new stock issue instead of a new debt issue. Now suppose that 30 percent of EFR would be debt and 70 percent would be equity. The computation of the new interest would be: (30% × EFR) × (15%). The total EFR would be added to the common stock and existing debt. This computation is shown in Figure 4.1.

Table 4.7
Delta Company Reconciled Balance Sheet

Cash	$ 24,000	Accounts Payable	$ 12,000
Marketable Securities	10,000	Accruals	4,800
Receivables	60,000	Notes Payable	-0-
Inventory	84,000	Total	16,800
Total	178,000		
Net Fixed Assets	184,000	Long-term Debt (Existing)	96,000
Total Assets	362,000	Long-term Debt (EFR)	67,300
		Common Stock	64,000
		Retained Earnings	117,900
		Total	$ 362,000

Figure 4.1
Reconciliation of the Income Statement and the Balance Sheet—30 Percent Debt to Equity Ratio

$$112,000 + 16,800 + 96,000 + EFR +$$
$$\{ [44,160 - 14,400 - (30\% \times EFR)(.15)] -$$
$$(EBT) [(1 - .5)(1 - .4)] \} = \$362,000$$

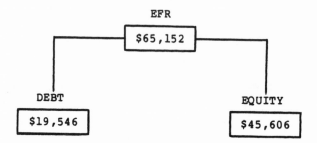

Overall Example

Using the percent of sales method, reasonable estimates for pro forma statements can be prepared, as shown in this example. In Table 4.8 a balance sheet and income statement appear for the Zeta Company. Using this information and the information in Table 4.9 about the following year, pro forma financial statements may be computed. The computations for the financial statements appear in Tables 4.10 and 4.11. The actual statements appear in Tables 4.12 and 4.13.

Table 4.8
Zeta Company 19X1 Balance Sheet and Income Statement

Cash	$ 10,000	Accounts Payable	$ 6,000
Marketable Securities	10,000	Taxes Payable	24,000
Accounts Receivable	20,000	Accruals	7,000
Inventory	70,000	Total	37,000
Total	110,000	Notes Payable (8%)	30,000
Building	200,000	Bonds Payable (12%)	60,000
Equipment	30,000	Common Stock	96,000
Total Assets	340,000	Retained Earnings	116,000
		Total	$ 340,000

Sales	$ 490,000
Cost of Goods Sold	- 290,000
Gross Profit	200,000
Selling and Admin. Expenses	- 120,000
EBIT	80,000
Interest*	- 9,600
EBT	70,400
Taxes (46%)	- 32,384
Net Income	38,016
Dividends	- 30,000
Additions to Retained Earnings	8,016

```
* 30,000 @ 8%  =  2400
  60,000 @ 12% =  7200
  Interest Exp.  9600
```

Table 4.9
Zeta Company 19X2 Changes

CHANGES IN 19X2

1. $50,000 sales increase

2. $10,000 new equipment required

3.   Building maintenance will offset depreciation

4.   45% of EFR to be financed with 10% debt

STEPS TO PREPARE PRO FORMA STATEMENTS

1.   Find new total assets

2.   Find pro forma EBIT

3.   Find EFR with reconciliation computation

4.   Complete income statement and balance sheet

Table 4.10
Computations for Financial Statements

Asset Computation

Cash	11,020
Marketable Securities	10,000
Receivables	22,040
Inventory	77,142
Total	120,202
Building	200,000
Equipment	40,000
Total Assets	360,202

Liabilities and Equity Computation

Accounts Payable	6,612
Taxes Payable	26,448
Accruals	7,714
Total	40,774
Notes Payable	30,000
Bonds Payable	60,000
Common Stock	96,000
Retained Earnings	$116,000

Table 4.10 (cont.)

EBIT Computation

Sales	$ 540,000
Cost of Goods Sold	319,680
Gross Profit	220,320
Selling and Admin.	
Expenses	132,300
EBIT	$ 88,020

Table 4.11
Zeta Company Reconciliation Computation

$$\$226,774 + 117,000 + EFR + 88,000 - 9,600 - (.45)(EFR)(.10)$$

$$(1 - .46)(1 - 15/19) = \$360,202$$

$$EFR = \underline{\$7,552}$$

Table 4.12
Zeta Company Pro Forma Balance Sheet

Cash	$ 11,020	Accounts Payable	$ 6,612
Marketable Securities	10,000	Taxes Payable	26,448
Receivables	22,040	Accruals	7,714
Inventory	77,142	Total	40,774
Total	120,202	Notes Payable	30,000
Building	200,000	Debt (EFR) (7,552 X .45)	3,398
Equipment	40,000	Bonds Payable	60,000
Total Assets	$360,202*	Common Stock	
		(96,000 + .55 X 7,552)	100,154
		Retained Earnings	125,830
		Total	$360,156*

*Rounding Difference

Table 4.13
Zeta Company Pro Forma Income Statement

Sales		$540,000
Cost of Goods Sold		⁻319,680
Gross Profit		220,320
Selling and Admin. Expenses		−132,300
EBIT		88,020
Interest - old	9600	
Interest - new	756	− 10,356
EBT		77,664
Taxes (46%)		− 35,726
Net Income		41,938
Dividends		− 33,108
Addition to Retained Earnings		8,830
Beginning Retained Earnings		117,000
Retained Earnings		$125,830

5

PRO FORMA APPLICATIONS

Once the basics of constructing pro formas are mastered, there are a number of useful applications that are possible. A good manager will latch on to every piece of information that comes along and squeeze out all the benefits possible. Pro formas are an excellent source of information for exploitation by a good manager. This chapter looks at some of the applications of pro forma statements. It covers some of the characteristics of three basic financial statements, reviews ratio analysis, and illustrates how the DuPont form of analysis might be used to aid in management decisions. Chapters 6 and 7 show how managers might evaluate growth prospects for a company.

USES OF FINANCIAL STATEMENTS

Financial statements are not always necessary to gauge management performance or for purposes of planning. Some managers can walk out into the plant, look at the product, talk to workers and customers, and get a good feel for how well they're doing. All those things may be true. In many cases, however, managers don't have that luxury. Managers of large conglomerates certainly don't have the time to walk out into all the plants they manage; nor can they talk to workers and customers. In these instances, managers must use whatever tools they do have at their disposal to generate information and to ascertain how well everyone concerned is performing.

In many cases, the best pieces of information available are the financial statements of the company, and they must be milked for all they're worth. Granted financial statements may not be the optimal sources of information managers might hope for, but many times they're the only source of information available. In that case, one has to overlook shortcomings and use the tools judiciously.

SHORTCOMINGS OF FINANCIAL STATEMENTS

One of the big shortcomings of financial statements is the fact that they're abstract representations of the ingredients that make a company what it is. For instance, assume that a company has a piece of tooling equipment that is vital to production. How might one convey all that piece of equipment means to the company? To write a treatise describing the equipment and its value to your company might take pages. To add up all the ingredients of what makes a company and generate such descriptions for each ingredient would result in a tome so thick that no one would have the time to read it. Instead some kind of "shorthand" system might be preferable. Of course users of the information will not get the full idea of the equipment (or any of the other ingredients of your company) from the shorthand version. Information content will be sacrificed for brevity. One might think of financial statements as a kind of shorthand version describing various ingredients. Financial statements are black-and-white representations of the value of business ingredients. In spite of the problems and shortcomings of financial statements, often they are the best information available and must be used for all they are worth.

THE BASIC FINANCIAL STATEMENTS

There are a number of financial statements that might be useful to managers. Among the basic ones that are common to most businesses, though, are the balance sheet, the income statement and the statement of changes in financial position. The balance sheet and the income statement have been covered in previous chapters; however, this is a good place to review some of their relevant characteristics for future use in management decisions. The statement of changes in financial position (sometimes called the funds statement) has not been covered, so it will be described in more detail.

The Balance Sheet

The balance sheet may be thought of as a statement describing the firm's financial health on a particular date. The reason it might be thought of in that manner is because the balance sheet details what a firm *owns* on that date and what it *owes*. What the firm owns are its assets; what it owes are the claims against those assets.

There are a number of factors to keep in mind about the balance sheet, having to do with balancing the statement, the order of listing, and how items are valued on the statement.

Balancing: The balance sheet has to balance; in other words, the assets of the company must equal the claims against those assets. The assets of the company are, of course, those things that the company owns. The claims against the company come from creditors (in the form of liabilities) and from owners (in the form of owners' equity).

Order of listing: Items on the balance sheet are listed in order of liquidity. For assets, liquidity means "nearness to cash." In valuing assets, then, one has to think of how quickly the company could raise money by selling off its assets. A treasury bond (a type of marketable security) could be sold off for cash quickly; therefore, it is a very liquid type of asset. In fact, it is second only to cash in terms of liquidity. By factoring its accounts receivable a company could raise cash, but not as quickly as it could by selling a marketable security. Next on the order of liquidity would be inventory. The fixed assets, like plant and equipment, would not be so liquid, so they are in another classification altogether.

For liabilities, liquidity takes on a slightly different shade of meaning. Liquidity for liabilities refers to how quickly the claim against the company will mature. Ordinary claims that arise during the normal course of business operations, such as accounts payable and accruals, will be listed first. Notes payable will probably mature next, so they're next on the list. Intermediate-term liabilities and longer-term liabilities (such as bonds, mortgages, and the like) appear next. Last claims to mature against a company of course are those of owners, so owners' equity accounts appear last on the claims side of the balance sheet.

Valuing of items: Assets are put on the balance sheet at their original cost. Exceptions are marketable securities and inventory. These items are listed at market value or cost, whichever figure is lower. One thing to keep in mind when it comes to land and buildings is that these are always separated, because buildings depreciate but land doesn't. Liabilities are listed on the balance sheet at the amount of the transaction.

The Income Statement

The income statement details the firm's revenues and the expenses and taxes associated with those revenues for some financial period. It might be easy to think of the income statement as showing what goes on at different levels, starting with the production level of the company. Revenues from operations will be listed, and then associated costs will be stripped away. Then the next level will be examined—the effects of selling and administrative costs will be noted—and so on down until the last level. This is where any dividends paid to shareholders are listed; whatever is left over after this final level is plowed back into the company in the form of retained earnings.

Statement of Changes in Financial Position (Funds Statement)

The statement of changes in financial position shows the sources and uses of funds for a company. In that sense, the funds statement can provide pretty good clues about how management is performing its job. Think about what management does in terms of the balance sheet. Everything on the liabilities and owners' equity side might be thought of as sources of funds for a company and everything on the assets side might be thought of as uses of funds for a company. For an illustration of this idea, refer to Figure 5.1. The sources of funds represent all the resources that management pulls into a company. To be successful, management should attract good sources of funds at a good rate. Once these funds are pulled into the company, management has a pool of resources available to it. It can put this pool of resources to work for the company. Everything that has to do with the sources of funds might be thought of as investing decisions for the firm and everything that has to do with the uses of funds might be thought of as investing decisions.

Regarding the pool of funds available for the company, management might decide to channel resources out of the pool to be put to work generating returns for the company. The company might decide to buy inventory to build a product, it might invest in government bonds, build a plant in New Jersey, or buy out a competitor. At any rate, the management of the company should attempt to put every dollar it brings into the company to work in a manner that will generate the greatest returns for the company. If a company performs these functions well, then there's probably a good management team on board.

If the performance of these functions could be monitored, then good clues to the quality of management could be gathered. One of the ways to get a feel for how well these functions are performed is through the funds statement.

Figure 5.1
Sources and Uses of Funds

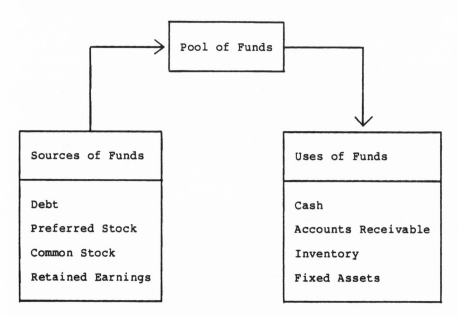

Example of Using Funds Statement. Perhaps the first step in understanding their effectiveness is to use an example. Assume that an analyst is examining two companies, Alpha and Beta, as potential investments. The analyst identifies the total assets for Alpha Company as $274 million and for Beta as $28 million. Although Alpha is clearly bigger than Beta, that does not necessarily mean that Alpha is better.

Looking at profits, the analyst sees that Alpha's current profits are $29 million and that Beta's are $3 million. Again, these figures do not necessarily mean that Alpha is better, only bigger.

Now the analyst looks at the sources and uses of funds (illustrated in Table 5.1). The chief sources of funds of Alpha are borrowed funds, for Beta retained earnings. The chief uses of funds for Alpha are dividends and paying off existing long-term debt. Beta's chief uses are the purchase of plant and equipment.

Now there is a real clue to discern the quality of the two companies. Beta appears to know where it is going. The company is making profits and plowing them back into the company. What is Beta doing with those resources? Expanding productive facilities. Just on the surface it looks like Beta is gearing up for growth. Alpha, on the other hand, looks like it's "borrowing from Peter to pay Paul." It is a big company, and it has obviously grown in the past. The present is a different story though.

Any analyst would want to dig further before making any investment decisions, and obviously our example just scratched the surface. It illustrated, however, just how useful the funds statement can be in getting at that fundamental job of management—the management of the sources and uses of funds.

Constructing a Funds Statement. Now it is important to understand how the statement is put together. There are a number of steps in constructing the funds statement:

1. Compare two balance sheets—a beginning and an ending balance sheet item.
2. Identify the changes between each item.
3. Classify those changes as to whether they're sources or uses of funds.
4. Assemble the information in desired format.
5. Analyze the information.

Table 5.1
Sources and Uses, Alpha and Beta Companies

	Alpha	Beta
Sources	Borrowed Funds	Retained Earnings
Uses	Dividends Reduction in long-term debt	Purchase Fixed Assets

Notice that step 3 is to classify changes as sources or uses of funds. That's actually quite simple. Anything that adds to the pool of resources is a source of funds and anything taken out of the pool is a use of funds. A simple decision rule might be employed:

Source of funds: Increase in a liability item
                 Decrease in an asset item

Use of funds: Increase in an asset item
              Decrease in a liability item

Using this, it is easy to classify changes as sources or uses of funds. Using the 19X1 and 19X2 balance sheets for Delta Company a funds statement could be drawn. Tables 5.2 and 5.3 are the balance sheets and Table 5.4 shows the changes between the balance sheet items and the classification of these changes.

Table 5.2
Delta Company 19X1 Balance Sheet

Cash	$ 20,000	Accounts Payable	$ 10,000
Mkt. Sec	10,000	Accruals	4,000
Receivables	50,000	Notes Payable	24,000
Inventory	70,000		
Fixed Assets	160,000	Long-Term Debt	96,000
		Common Stock	64,000
		Retained Earnings	112,000
TOTAL	310,000	TOTAL	310,000

Table 5.3
Delta Company 19X1 Balance Sheet

Cash	$ 5,000	Accounts Payable	$ 10,000
Mkt. Sec	10,000	Accruals	4,000
Receivables	5,145	Notes Payable	-0-
Inventory	32,250		
Fixed Assets	172,000	Long-Term Debt	2,720
		Common Stock	64,000
		Retained Earnings	143,675
TOTAL	224,395	TOTAL	224,395

Table 5.4
Projected Funds Statement Step 1, Delta Company 19X2

	19X2	19X1	Source	Use
Cash	$ 5,000	$ 20,000	$ 15,000	
Mkt. Sec	10,000	10,000		
Receivables	5,145	50,000	44,805	
Inventory	32,250	70,000	37,750	
Fixed Assets	172,000	160,000		12,000
Accounts Payable	10,000	10,000		
Accruals	4,000	4,000		
Notes Payable	-0-	24,000		24,000
Long-Term Debt	2,720	96,000		93,280
Common Stock	64,000	64,000		
Retained Earnings	143,675	112,000	31,675	
TOTAL			129,280	129,280

At the end of 19X1, cash was $20,000. If things work out the way Delta plans, cash at the end of 19X2 will be $5,000. The difference, $15,000, is a reduction in an asset item. According to the decision rule, a decrease in an asset item is a source of funds.

That a reduction in cash is a source of funds might bother some people. This seeming paradox, however, results from the particular manner in which sources and uses of funds are defined. Remember, sources and uses of funds refer to that pool of resources available to the company. A company can bring funds into the firm using a number of alternatives: It may borrow money, may obtain from owners by selling stock, or may plow profits back into the company. Anything that increases the size of that pool is a source of funds.

Then managers look at that pool of funds and make decisions on how to put the funds to work. They might buy inventory, invest in C.D.s, or they might decide to deposit the money in a checking account. By building up the bank balance, they make a use of funds. Another way to look at it is to say that money can go in the bank or it can be put to some alternative use. Therefore, a reduction in cash would be a source of funds. The rest of the balance sheet changes can be classified as in Table 5.4. Once changes are classified, then total sources and total uses should be summed; and they should balance, as they do in this case. If they do not, an error is present and must be corrected.

Next, the statement should be constructed. The format depends in large part on what is to be done with the statement. If the statement is to be prepared for external use—for stockholders, lenders, or the like—then a formal statement of changes in financial position should be prepared according to accepted accounting rules and principles. An accountant can assist in this preparation. Table 5.5 illustrates how such a statement might appear. This chapter concentrates on managerial applications, however, so such a statement will not actually be constructed.

If the statement is to be used internally, for gauging company performance and similar uses, then a less formal statement can be employed. A simple funds statement is all that is needed. Some managers leave the information in the form shown in Table 5.4, and then go ahead with their analysis. Some rework the

Table 5.5
Statement of Changes in Financial Position, Delta Company

```
Sources of Funds

       Net Income From Operations              $  41,675*

       Reduction in Cash                          15,000

       Reduction in Receivables                   44,855

       Reduction in Inventory                     37,750

       Depreciation                               10,000**

Total Sources of Funds                         $149,280


Uses of Funds

       Increase in Fixed Assets               $  22,000**

       Decrease in Notes Payable                  24,000

       Increase in Long-Term Debt                 93,280

       Dividends                                  10,000*

Total Uses of Funds                            $149,280
```

* In this case, the statement shows changes in retained earnings (a source of $31,675) broken down as net income from operations (a source of $41,675) less dividends ($10,000 use).

** Statement shows $12,000 change in fixed assets as $22,000 (use) less $10,000 change in depreciation (source).

information and list total sources and total uses separately. In that case, it might be helpful to organize total sources and total uses with the largest item in each group appearing first. Other items in each group should then be listed in descending magnitude. This organization helps when it comes time to analyze the statement. An example of such a statement for Delta appears in Table 5.6

Analyzing Results. The key in analyzing a funds statement is to identify the flow of funds through the firm and see if and how well management is doing its job. How does it bring money into the company, and how does it put those funds to work? Table 5.7 illustrates a funds statement for Alpha Company.

Table 5.6
Projected Funds Statement Step 2, Delta Company 19X2

Sources of Funds

Reduction in Accounts Receivables	$ 44,855	
Reduction in Inventory	37,750	
Retained Earnings	31,675	
Reduction in Cash	15,000	
Total Sources of Funds		$129,280

Uses of Funds

Payoff Long-Term Liabilities	$ 93,280	
Payoff Notes Payable	24,000	
Purchase Fixed Assets	12,000	
Total Uses of Funds		$129,280

Table 5.7
Funds Statement, Alpha Company

Sources of Funds

Increase in Long-term Debt	$38,300
Increase in Accounts Payable	22,100
Reduction in Inventory	12,300
Retained Earnings	8,300
Total Sources	$81,000

Uses of Funds

Accounts Receivables	$47,080
Increase in Inventory	32,135
Increase in Cash	1,785
Total Uses	$81,000

Looking at chief funds for the company, it is evident that borrowed funds serve as the chief source of funds for Alpha. Debt, although perhaps a cheap form of capital, is a risky form of capital. If Alpha becomes debt-laden, then it runs the risk of not being able to repay the debt. It runs increased risk of being in default and even of bankruptcy.

Looking at the uses of funds for Alpha, the chief use is a substantial increase in accounts receivable. Note that this increase occurred without a corresponding increase in profits. Therefore it appears that collection of receivables is faltering. The next largest use of funds is inventory. It would be wise to check immediately to see if this increase was in finished goods inventory. If that is the case, then such a buildup in inventory portends gloom for Alpha. This indicates a problem in sales. By now, the point should be clear. Alpha is having problems. The point is to look at each item, then put the whole picture together to get clues about what is behind the numbers. In this case, it should be evident that Alpha needs to take some immediate action to correct problems before they get any more out of control.

Back to Delta: Table 5.6 illustrates a funds statement organized with largest sources and uses. Delta is paying off a great deal of debt, obtaining some productive equipment, and using short-term assets to fund these moves. All in all, it appears that Delta is probably doing all right. It is clear that the important thing in utilizing financial statements is to get behind the numbers. Ratio analysis is another tool that allows managers to get behind the numbers.

RATIO ANALYSIS

One of the ways in which financial statements can be put to work is through ratio analysis. Ratios are simply one number divided by another number; as such, they may or may not be meaningful. In finance, ratios are usually two financial statement items that may be related to one another and may provide the prudent user a good deal of information. There are tens of thousands of ratios that could be generated, some more meaningful than others. Generally ratios are divided into four areas of classification that provide different kinds of information: liquidity, turnover, profitablity, and debt.

Classification of Ratios

Figures 5.2–5.6 illustrate the areas of classification and some useful ratios in each area. Obviously, pro formas can be utilized in the same fashion. The resulting ratios can provide a basis for planning and decision making. Table 5.9 shows ratios calculated for Delta based on Tables 5.3 and 5.8.

Figure 5.2
Abbreviations Used in Ratios

CA:	Current Assets	COGS:	Cost of Goods Sold
CL:	Current Liabilities	GP:	Gross Profits
INV:	Inventory	NI:	Net Income
TA:	Total Assets	OE:	Owner's Equity
FA:	Fixed Assets	TL:	Total Liabilities

Figure 5.3
Liquidity Ratios

LIQUIDITY RATIOS - Indicate the firm's ability to meet its maturing short-term obligations.

A. Current Ratio $\dfrac{CA}{CL}$ - Indicates how many times current assets cover current liabilities.

B. Quick Ratio $\dfrac{CA - INV}{CL}$ - Indicates how many times quick assets cover current liabilities.

Figure 5.4
Turnover Ratios

TURNOVER RATIOS - Indicate how effectively the firm manages resources at its disposal to generate sales.

C. Total Asset Turnover $\dfrac{Sales}{TA}$ - Indicates the effectiveness of the firm in generating sales by utilizing total assets.

D. Fixed Asset Turnover $\dfrac{SALES}{FA}$ - Indicates the effectiveness of the firm in generating sales by utilizing its fixed assets.

E. Inventory Turnover $\dfrac{Sales}{INV}$ - Indicates how effectively the firm utilized its inventory to generate sales.

Figure 5.5
Profitability Ratios

PROFITABILITY RATIOS - Indicate the efficiency of management.

- F. Inventory Turnover (CGS) $\dfrac{COGS}{INV}$ - Indicates the firm's effectiveness in managing its inventory.

- G. Gross Profit Margin $\dfrac{GP}{Sales}$ - Indicates overall effectiveness of management.

- H. Net Profit Margin $\dfrac{NI}{Sales}$ - Indicates "bottom-line" effectiveness.

- I. Return on Assets $\dfrac{NI}{TA}$ - Relates profitability of assets.

- J. Return on Equity $\dfrac{NI}{OE}$ - Indicates returns to shareholders.

Figure 5.6
Debt Ratios

DEBT RATIOS - Indicates the extent to which the firm is financed by debt.

- K. Debt Ratio $\dfrac{TL}{TA}$ - Indicates the percentage of
  total capital financed by debt.

Table 5.8
Delta Company Pro Forma Income Statement

Sales	$240,000
Cost of Goods Sold	140,750
Gross Profits	99,250
Selling & Administrative Costs	27,500
Earnings Before Interest & Taxes	71,750
Interest *	8,400
Earnings Before Taxes	63,350
Taxes **	31,675
NET INCOME	31,675

* Based on last year's interest cost. As Delta goes through the planning process, it may want to adjust this amount, should it decide to seek additional financing or pay off old debt.

** Assuming 50 percent taxes

Table 5.9
Ratio Analysis, Delta Company (Based on Tables 5.3 and 5.8)

A. Current Ratio: $\dfrac{\text{CA:}}{\text{CL}}$ $\dfrac{52,395}{14,000}$ = 3.74 X

B. Quick: $\dfrac{\text{CA-INV:}}{\text{CL}}$ $\dfrac{52,395-32,250}{14,000}$ = 1.44 X

C. Total Asset Turnover: $\dfrac{\text{Sales}}{\text{TA}}$ = $\dfrac{240,000}{224,395}$ = 1.07 X

D. Fixed Asset Turnover: $\dfrac{\text{Sales}}{\text{FA}}$ = $\dfrac{240,000}{172,000}$ = 1.39 X

E. Inventory Turnover: $\dfrac{\text{Sales}}{\text{INV}}$ = $\dfrac{240,000}{32,250}$ = 7.44 X

F. Inventory Turnover (CGS): $\dfrac{\text{COGS}}{\text{INV}}$ = $\dfrac{140,750}{32,250}$ = 4.36 X

G. Gross Profit Margin: $\dfrac{\text{GP}}{\text{Sales}}$ = $\dfrac{99,250}{240,000}$ = 41.3%

H. Net Profit Margin: $\dfrac{\text{NI}}{\text{Sales}}$ = $\dfrac{31,675}{240,000}$ = 13.2%

I. Return on Assets: $\dfrac{\text{NI}}{\text{TA}}$ = $\dfrac{31,675}{224,395}$ = 14.1%

J. Return on Equity: $\dfrac{\text{NI}}{\text{OE}}$ = $\dfrac{31,675}{207,675}$ = 15.2%

K. Debt Ratio: $\dfrac{\text{TL}}{\text{TA}}$ = $\dfrac{16,720}{224,395}$ = 7.4%

Evaluations

Remember, ratios are just one number divided by another number and as such really don't mean much. The trick is in the way ratios are analyzed and used by the decision maker. A good strategy is to compare the ratios to some sort of benchmark, such as industry averages or to what a company has done in the past, or both.

Interpretation of Ratios

How does the analyst "get behind the numbers"? An example might be the best way to illustrate. Assume that it is necessary to analyze management performance, but there is a real shortage of information. All that is known is that the company has a current ratio of 5.93 and a quick ratio of 1.89. That is not a lot of information and no competent analyst can make solid recommendations based on such a dearth of information. Yet there is one observation that can be made: the company has a lot tied up in inventory. This situation is not necessarily bad or good—it just depends on the circumstances. Until further information is available no judgments should be made; but it is possible to reflect on what might be going on in the company. To organize such reflections, it might be helpful to look at bad reasons for such an inventory buildup, then good ones.

It is possible that the company has a buildup in inventory because of slippages in sales. If that is the case, a number of factors could be responsible for sales declines. The company may have done a poor job of sales forecasting. The product may be nearing the end of its life cycle. Maybe quality control is slipping and customers are expressing dissatisfaction by not buying the product.

The buildup might be in work-in-process or finished goods inventory. There may be flaws in the production process or the ordering process in such a case. There may be a host of other "bad" reasons for such a buildup in inventory, but by now the message is probably clear. A good manager can look at numbers and "brainstorm" about what may be causing those numbers. On to the "good" reasons.

A company may have a buildup in inventory, but the buildup may have been planned. For instance, a company may build up inventory of increased sales demands due to seasonal or cyclical fluctuations. It may build up inventory in anticipation of a strike by the company's workers or supplier's workers. It might build up inventory in order to take advantage of anticipated price hikes or the like. Again, the point is probably clear. Just by looking at two numbers—the current and quick ratios—a good manager can conjecture about all the possible causes. A good manager might even come up with solutions for problems that might exist. Certainly, no judgment or plan should be formulated until further information is available, but this example does illustrate how a skillful manager "gets behind" the numbers. Financial statements as well as pro forma statements might be scrutinized.

COMPARISONS

Once ratios are calculated, an analyst needs some benchmarks to find out where the company stands at that particular point. Useful benchmarks are industry comparisons and company trends.

Industry Comparisons

It may be useful to compare a company to certain industry averages to get a feel for how the company is performing. In that case it is necessary to obtain industry performance measures. There are a number of sources of industry figures:

1. *Commercial sources*: A number of companies publish information on industry comparisons. Among these sources are private credit reporting agencies such as Dun and Bradstreet and Robert Morris and Associates. Rating agencies such as Moody's and Standard and Poor's also provide industry information. Addresses for these companies appear in Appendix B.
2. *Government sources*: There are a number of government sources of helpful industry information. These range from calculated ratios to industry outlooks. Some sources are listed in Appendix B.
3. *Trade associations*: Many industries have trade associations or industry groups that regularly publish information for and about members. This information might prove useful in industry comparisons.

Once industry measures are obtained, then an analyst can compare individual company figures to the average for the industry, the top performers, the worst performers, or whatever is deemed suitable.

Table 5.10 contains some industry averages for Delta's industry. Examples of using industry averages appear in Figures 5.7–5.17 and Table 5.11. Using these figures as benchmarks, an analyst might make comparisons and arrive at

Table 5.10
Industry Averages

A.	Current Ratio	2.38
B.	Quick Ratio	1.12
C.	Total Asset Turnover	1.05
D.	Fixed Asset Turnover	1.02
E.	Inventory Turnover	7.89
F.	Inventory Turnover (CGS)	4.54
G.	Gross Profit Margin	37.6%
H.	Net Profit Margin	11.2%
I.	Return on Assets	12.8%
J.	Return on Equity	13.9%
K.	Debt Ratio	32.7%

Table 5.11
Industry and Delta Averages Compared

RATIO	INDUSTRY	DELTA	ANALYSIS
Current Ratio	2.38	3.74	Well Above
Quick Ratio	1.12	1.44	Above
Total Asset Turnover	1.05	1.07	Average
Fixed Asset Turnover	1.02	1.39	Above
Inventory Turnover	7.89	7.44	Below
Inventory Turnover (CGS)	4.54	4.36	Below
Gross Profit Margin	37.6%	41.3%	Above
Net Profit Margin	11.2%	13.2%	Well Above
Return on Assets	12.8%	14.1%	Well Above
Return on Equity	13.9%	15.2%	Well Above
Debt Ratio	32.7%	7.4%	Well Below

Figure 5.7
Current Ratio

Industry: 2.38	Delta: 3.74

Delta is higher than industry average. This can be good
or bad. On the one hand, Delta is more cushioned than
average against short-term working capital needs.

On the other hand, this shows Delta has more funds than
average tied up in current assets. It may wish to channel
some of these funds into greater return generating assets.

Figure 5.8
Quick Ratio

```
Industry: 1.12                    Delta: 1.44
```

Delta is still higher than industry standard, indicating
again a cushion against short-term working capital needs.
Note, however, difference in quick ratio is not so great
as difference in current ratio. This indicates a somewhat
greater buildup in inventory for Delta. See discussion
earlier in chapter on inventory buildups.

Figure 5.9
Total Asset Turnover

```
Industry: 1.05                    Delta: 1.07
```

Delta is average for industry.

Figure 5.10
Fixed Asset Turnover

```
Industry: 1.02                    Delta: 1.39
```

Delta is above industry average. Note that it was average
in total asset turnover. Total asset turnover indicates
performance in managing fixed assets and current assets.
Good fixed asset performance and average total asset
performance mean there may be a slippage in current
asset management.

Figure 5.11
Inventory Turnover

```
┌─────────────────────────────────────────────────┐
│ Industry: 7.89                    Delta: 7.44     │
└─────────────────────────────────────────────────┘
```

Delta is below industry average. This may indicate an
inventory management problem. This would account for
slippage in current asset management indicated in two
previous figures.

Figure 5.12
Inventory Turnover (CGS)

```
┌─────────────────────────────────────────────────┐
│ Industry: 4.54                    Delta: 4.36     │
└─────────────────────────────────────────────────┘
```

Again, Delta is below average. This confirms an inventory
management problem.

Figure 5.13
Gross Profit Margin

```
┌─────────────────────────────────────────────────┐
│ Industry: 37.6%                   Delta: 41.3%    │
└─────────────────────────────────────────────────┘
```

Delta is slightly higher than industry average.

Figure 5.14
Net Profit Margin

```
┌─────────────────────────────────────────────────┐
│ Industry: 11.2%                   Delta: 13.2%    │
└─────────────────────────────────────────────────┘
```

Delta is performing better than average. This compared to
gross profit performance provides some indication that Delta
is managing general and administrative types of expenses
well.

Figure 5.15
Return on Assets

```
┌─────────────────────────────────────────────────────────┐
│  Industry: 12.8%                          Delta: 14.1%    │
└─────────────────────────────────────────────────────────┘
```

Delta is performing better than average for industry. This
should enhance stockholder perception.

Figure 5.16
Return on Equity

```
┌─────────────────────────────────────────────────────────┐
│  Industry: 13.9%                          Delta: 15.2%    │
└─────────────────────────────────────────────────────────┘
```

Again, Delta's doing a good job and stockholders are likely
to be satisfied with such performance.

Figure 5.17
Debt Ratio

```
┌─────────────────────────────────────────────────────────┐
│  Industry: 32.7%                          Delta: 7.4%     │
└─────────────────────────────────────────────────────────┘
```

Delta is well below the industry average. On the one hand
it minimizes risk. On the other hand, though, it may be
sacrificing potential returns to shareholders. See Chapter
6 for an extended discussion of debt considerations.

certain judgments. These judgments are strictly arbitrary and depend on the experience, wisdom, and judgment of the analyst. There are a number of factors to keep in mind when making industry comparisons, however:

1. It is okay to compare an individual company to the industry average, but remember that most of the companies in the industry may be poor performers. Frankly, there are a lot of industries in the United States that have less-than-farsighted management and are woefully behind times. Comparing an individual company to the average for such an industry might mean that the company would settle for less-than-optimal performance. A company should always keep in mind that it is okay to reap average performance for an industry, but it is better sometimes to forget about the competition and just be the best that a company can be.

2. There may be significant reporting differences in industry averages. For instance, when looking at an item that utilizes inventory as an input it must be remembered that some companies may use LIFO (last in, first out), some may use FIFO, and so on. Therefore it is necessary to use industry figures judiciously.

3. Within an industry, there may be companies of many sizes. Some sources of data, such as Robert Morris, adjust for size differences. This is important. It would not be reasonable to assume that small companies would have the same ratios as very large companies.

4. In addition to an industry analysis, it is always helpful to look at a trend analysis.

Trend Analysis

A trend analysis is useful in making the determinations of where a company has been and where it is going. An example of performing a trend analysis appears in Tables 5.12–5.22 and Figures 5.18–5.28.

Table 5.12
Trend Data, Current Ratio

	4 Yrs Ago	3 Yrs Ago	2 Yrs Ago	1 Yr Ago	Pro Forma
Current Assets	169,834	171,880	172,000	150,000	52,395
Current Liabilities	40,100	42,100	43,000	38,000	14,000
Current Ratio	4.73	4.08	4.00	3.94	3.74

Figure 5.18
Trend Analysis, Current Ratio

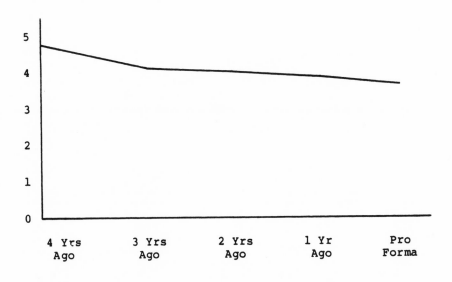

Table 5.13
Trend Data, Quick Ratio

	4 Yrs Ago	3 Yrs Ago	2 Yrs Ago	1 Yr Ago	Pro Forma
Current Assets	169,834	171,880	172,000	150,000	52,395
Inventory	61,834	62,000	68,000	70,000	32,250
Current Liabilities	40,100	42,100	43,000	38,000	14,000
Current Ratio	2.69	2.61	2.42	2.11	1.44

Figure 5.19
Trend Analysis, Quick Ratio

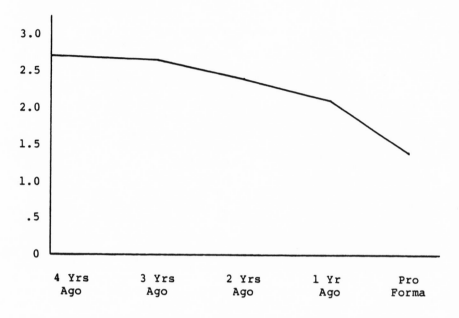

Table 5.14
Trend Data, Total Asset Turnover

	4 Yrs Ago	3 Yrs Ago	2 Yrs Ago	1 Yr Ago	Pro Forma
Sales	177,943	179,932	189,145	200,000	240,000
Total Assets	288,343	289,754	308,143	310,000	244,395
Total Asset Turnover	.62	.63	.61	.65	1.07

Figure 5.20
Trend Analysis, Total Asset Turnover

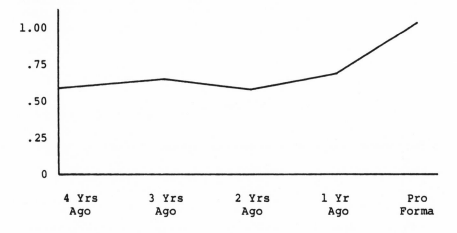

	4 Yrs Ago	3 Yrs Ago	2 Yrs Ago	1 Yr Ago	Pro Forma

Table 5.15
Trend Data, Fixed Asset Turnover

	4 Yrs Ago	3 Yrs Ago	2 Yrs Ago	1 Yr Ago	Pro Forma
Sales	177,943	179,932	189,145	200,000	240,000
Fixed Assets	156,843	157,125	158,933	160,000	172,000
Fixed Asset Turnover	1.13	1.15	1.19	1.25	1.39

Figure 5.21
Trend Analysis, Fixed Asset Turnover

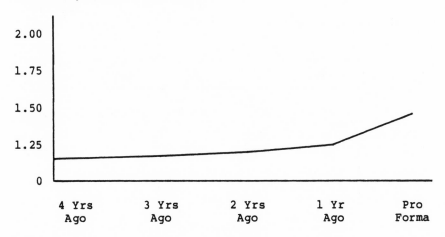

	4 Yrs Ago	3 Yrs Ago	2 Yrs Ago	1 Yr Ago	Pro Forma

Table 5.16
Trend Data, Inventory Turnover

	4 Yrs Ago	3 Yrs Ago	2 Yrs Ago	1 Yr Ago	Pro Forma
Sales	177,943	179,932	189,145	200,000	240,000
Inventory	66,972	67,945	68,123	70,000	32,250
Inventory Turnover	2.67	2.65	2.78	2.86	7.44

Figure 5.22
Trend Analysis, Inventory Turnover

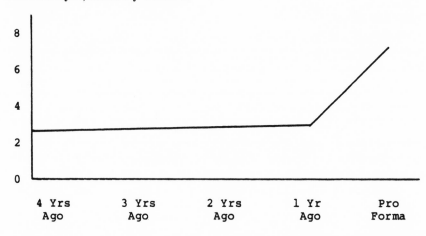

Table 5.17
Trend Data, Inventory Turnover (CGS)

	4 Yrs Ago	3 Yrs Ago	2 Yrs Ago	1 Yr Ago	Pro Forma
CGS	88,243	87,000	89,000	110,000	140,750
Inventory	66,972	67,945	68,123	70,000	32,250
Inventory Turnover (CGS)	1.32	1.28	1.31	1.57	4.36

Figure 5.23
Trend Analysis, Inventory Turnover (CGS)

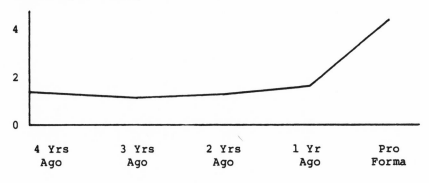

Table 5.18
Trend Data, Gross Profit Margin

	4 Yrs Ago	3 Yrs Ago	2 Yrs Ago	1 Yr Ago	Pro Forma
Gross Profits	87,123	86,110	88,143	90,000	99,250
Sales	177,943	179,932	189,145	200,000	240,000
GPM	48.9%	47.9%	46.6%	45.0%	41.3%

Figure 5.24
Trend Analysis, Gross Profit Margin

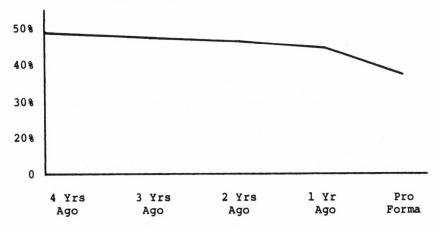

Table 5.19
Trend Data, Net Profit Margin

	4 Yrs Ago	3 Yrs Ago	2 Yrs Ago	1 Yr Ago	Pro Forma
Net Income	9,789	9,877	9,943	10,000	31,675
Sales	177,943	179,932	189,145	200,000	240,000
NPM	5.50%	5.49%	5.26%	5.00%	13.20%

Figure 5.25
Trend Analysis, Net Profit Margin

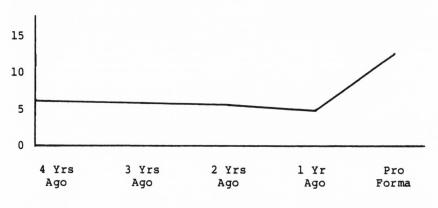

Table 5.20
Trend Data, Return on Assets

	4 Yrs Ago	3 Yrs Ago	2 Yrs Ago	1 Yr Ago	Pro Forma
Net Income	9,789	9,877	9,943	10,000	31,675
Total Assets	288,343	289,754	308,143	310,000	244,395
ROA	3.39%	3.41%	3.23%	3.20%	14.10%

Figure 5.26
Trend Analysis, Return on Assets

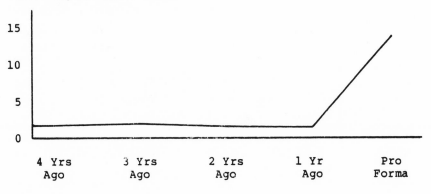

Table 5.21
Trend Data, Return on Equity

	4 Yrs Ago	3 Yrs Ago	2 Yrs Ago	1 Yr Ago	Pro Forma
Net Income	9,789	9,877	9,943	10,000	31,675
Owners' Equity	170,991	171,845	172,000	176,000	207,675
ROE	5.73%	5.75%	5.78%	5.68%	15.20%

Figure 5.27
Trend Analysis, Return on Equity

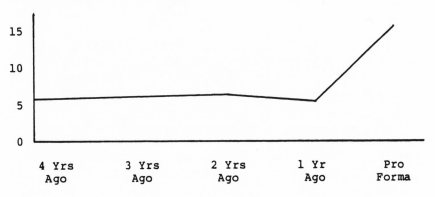

Table 5.22
Trend Data, Debt Ratio

	4 Yrs Ago	3 Yrs Ago	2 Yrs Ago	1 Yr Ago	Pro Forma
Total Liabilities	127,154	127,732	128,754	134,000	16,720
Total Assets	288,343	289,754	308,143	310,000	244,395
Debt Ratio	44.10%	44.08%	41.78%	43.23%	7.40%

Figure 5.28
Trend Analysis, Debt Ratio

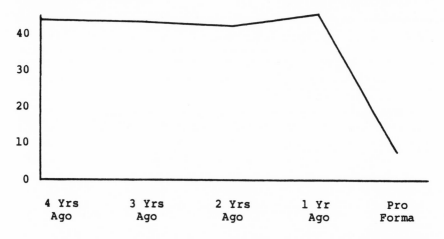

DUPONT ANALYSIS

There is another way to approach ratio analysis, and many professionals involved in finance consider this alternative approach to be more orderly. It is called DuPont analysis. Basically, DuPont analysis starts with a single ratio and branches out from there. Consider what an analyst would do if trying to pinpoint a single criterion of management performance. That analyst would want a ratio that would reflect management efficiency as well as its ability to generate sales (turnover). One ratio that fills that bill is return on total assets—net profits divided by total assets. Note that this ratio contains elements from both the balance sheet as well as the income statement. How might a manager use the DuPont ratio for purposes of analysis?

By looking at one scenario that illustrates the process, ideas on other situations in which this type of analysis is appropriate might be generated. Suppose the manager of a big conglomerate has control of 1,389 different divisions across the country. That manager certainly can't visit each division very often; as a matter of fact, the manager can't afford to devote much management time to any of the divisions. Therefore, the manager has to make every minute count. How will the manager identify developing problems? If there are adverse factors that might develop into big problems in any division, they must be identified as quickly as possible and nipped in the bud.

The manager gets financial statements every month, but the amount of time that may be spent analyzing them is limited. One solution is to rely on a DuPont approach. Instead of calculating numerous ratios, just start with one: the return on total assets. If the manager checks the return on total assets for each of the 1,389 divisions and nothing looks out of order, then go on to a bigger problem. If the manager notices that the return on total assets for one division is slipping, however, more time is needed to analyze the situation.

If the return on total assets is slipping, then the division has an efficiency problem, a turnover problem, or both. The next step is to check an overall efficiency ratio and an overall turnover ratio. (This is a good time to refer to Figure 5.28.) The overall efficiency ratio is the net profit margin and the overall turnover ratio is the total asset turnover. If total asset turnover looks good, then management time should be devoted to running down the efficiency problem. If there is an efficiency problem, then either sales are too low or costs are too high. The manager then needs to find out which and figure out what to do about it. If net profit margin looks good, then there is a turnover problem. If there is a total asset turnover problem, then it is a problem with fixed assets, current assets, or both.

The next step is to check the fixed asset turnover ratio. If it looks fine, then there is a problem with current assets, and vice-versa. It is up to the manager to identify the problems and figure out what to do about them, but it is apparent that DuPont analysis is a logical shortcut to ask the right questions and get to problem areas quickly. Table 5.23 and Figure 5.29 illustrate such a process for Beta Company. What about Delta? Using the ratios already calculated, a DuPont analysis might be accomplished as in Table 5.24 and Figure 5.30.

USES OF FINANCIAL STATEMENT INFORMATION

It should be apparent that good managers might use analytical techniques outlined in planning. Clues from analysis of funds statements and ratio analysis might be used in allocating resources, planning asset usage, and projecting sources of financing. Some of the following chapters illustrate such considerations. Not only should it be apparent that managers can use such tools internally, it is necessary to point out that others outside the company are also likely to utilize such tools and techniques. Investors and potential investors will be scrutinizing financial statements and comparing them to some benchmark. Creditors

Table 5.23
DuPont Analysis, Beta Company (Basic Information)

Assume you have information that details certain industry averages:

RATIO	INDUSTRY	BETA
Current Ratio	10.383	10.595
Quick Ratio	5.712	5.595
Total Asset Turnover	1.045	.663
Fixed Asset Turnover	2.012	1.304
Net Profit Margin	.042	.041
Return on Assets	.038	.027

Table 5.24
DuPont Analysis, Delta Company (Basic Information)

Assume you have information that details certain industry averages:

RATIO	INDUSTRY	BETA
Current Ratio	2.38	3.74
Quick Ratio	1.12	1.44
Total Asset Turnover	1.05	1.07
Fixed Asset Turnover	1.02	1.39
Net Profit Margin	11.2%	13.2%
Return on Assets	12.8%	14.1%

will analyze financial statements to determine whether a company is a good credit risk. It is necessary for managers to understand that even if they don't particularly care what their company's ratios look like, others do.

In other words, even if a company knows where it is headed, even if it is "on program," it still has to look at financial statements through the eyes of investors and creditors. Oftentimes in doing so, managers may find that their statements may look more attractive by cosmetic changes afforded by simple accounting transfers or the like. This might result in huge savings in costs of bringing capital into the company.

Figure 5.29
DuPont Analysis, Beta Company (Analysis of Information)

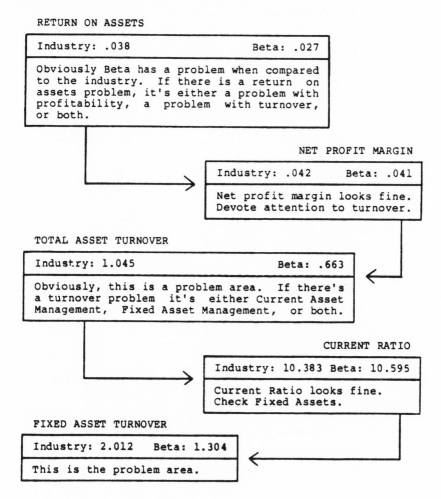

By using pro forma statements, calculating ratios, and analyzing the information, managers can often prevent problems before they occur. For instance, in analysis of pro forma ratios, management might note that returns to shareholders are too small. By going back and examining and correcting cost problems, they can enhance stockholder returns, heading off stockholder dissatisfaction before it occurs. The prevention of problems is the most useful application of ratio analysis.

Figure 5.30
DuPont Analysis, Delta Company (Analysis of Information)

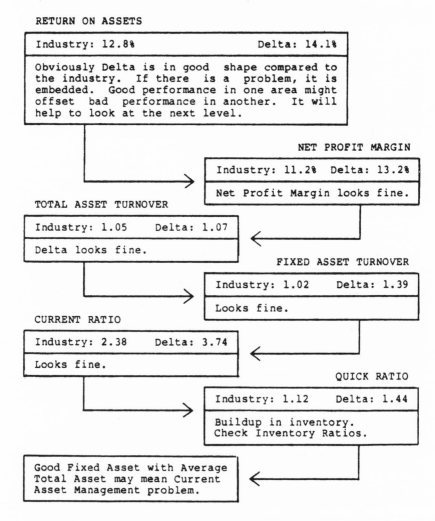

___ 6 ___

THE USE OF DEBT

Chapter 5 explored a number of managerial issues, including an extensive discussion of management of the sources and uses of funds or capital available to a firm. As covered in Chapter 5, it is evident that the procurement of funds for a firm involves decisions of paramount importance. This chapter explores at length some of the factors involved in the procurement of funds. In particular, the impact of debt financing is covered. Essentially, a firm has two broad choices in obtaining funds—debt or equity. Debt sources, of course, represent borrowed funds. Equity sources (preferred stock, common stock, retained earnings) represent funds raised from owners of the firm. Any choice of funds, of course, carries with it certain implications for management as well as for shareholders.

CHOICE OF FINANCING

Any time the management of a firm seeks to raise new funds, there are a number of issues that must be addressed: control, legal issues, tax considerations, and cost of financing.

Control: When investors give up their funds for someone else's use, they demand certain things in order to compensate for their loss of use of those funds. One of the things they demand, of course, is a just return on their investment. In addition, they also may demand other things. For instance, creditors may demand certain concessions. They may require that the company obtain their permission before raising any money in the future. They may demand sinking fund deposits in order to insure the company will have enough funds to cover the debt obligation at maturity. They may even demand the right to approve new top management.

Owners of the company may also demand certain things of the company before they buy stock in a company. Common stockholders are afforded the right to vote on important matters before the company. They have the right to inspect the company's books, the right to annual reports, and the like. These are only a few of the control issues that must be considered by a firm when it seeks new funds. Regardless of which form of funds on which a company relies, it must address all these control issues.

Legal Issues: There are a number of legal issues to be considered when raising funds. The company must comply with its corporate charter, any existing debt agreements, national laws, state laws, and the regulations of various agencies such as the Securities Exchange Commission.

Tax Considerations: Tax status of the firm and stockholders often affects any financing decision. One of the major factors to be considered is that interest payments on debt are tax deductible to the firm, whereas dividend payments are not. An outcome of this is that debt is most likely the cheapest form of financing available to the firm.

Cost of Financing: Generally, the firm must look at the cost of generating additional funds. Obviously, because of tax implications, debt is usually the cheapest form of capital available to the company. However, in incurring greater amounts of debt, the firm must be cognizant that additional debt affects investor perceptions of the company. Therefore, the firm must take into consideration the implications of debt financing from an investor viewpoint.

IMPLICATIONS OF DEBT FINANCING

Any time a firm seeks to raise funds, it must be aware that its actions may affect investor perceptions of the company. This includes both present and potential investors in the firm. Among investor concerns might be the risk of default on the part of the company and the risk of bankruptcy. At some point investors may become quite concerned about these eventualities. In order to compensate for this added concern, investors might demand added returns. This will affect the company in increased cost of borrowing, as well as adverse effects on the market value of the company's stocks. It is important that the company understand these potential factors any time it raises capital. It must also have a sense for when it is that investors may be overly concerned about risks. For this reason it is helpful for managers to get a feel for the impact of debt on the firm's financial statements.

HOW TO MEASURE IMPACT OF DEBT

First it is helpful to look at some miscellaneous balance sheet measures, and then at a measure of financial leverage.

Miscellaneous Measures

There are a couple of ratios that are helpful in gauging the impact of debt on the balance sheet: the debt ratio and the times interest earned ratio. In going over these ratios it is helpful to refer to Tables 6.1 and 6.2, Delta's balance sheet and income statement as reproduced from Chapter 3. The debt ratio was covered in Chapter 5, where it was suggested that the debt ratio be compared to industry benchmarks. What if a company has a great deal more debt than average for the industry? Is that necessarily bad? It must be remembered that debt can be the cheapest form of capital, so a higher than average debt ratio is in and of itself no cause for concern.

What is cause for concern is of course investor perceptions. When the debt ratio becomes so high that investors start worrying about risk of default and risk

Table 6.1
Delta Company 19X1 Balance Sheet

Cash	$ 20,000	Accounts Payable	$ 10,000
Marketable Securities	10,000	Accruals	4,000
Receivables	50,000	Notes Payable @ 10%	24,000
Inventory	70,000	Total	$ 38,000
Total	$150,000	Long-term Debt @ 15%	96,000
Net Fixed Assets	160,000	Common Stock	64,000
		Retained Earnings	112,000
Total Assets	$310,000	Total	$310,000

Table 6.2
Delta Company 19X1 Income Statement

	$
Sales	200,000
Cost of Goods Sold	- 110,000
Gross Profit	90,000
Selling and Admin. Expenses	- 53,200
EBIT	36,800
Interest	- 16,800
EBT	20,000
Taxes (50%)	- 10,000
Net Income	10,000

Table 6.3
Times Interest Earned

```
TIE =           EBIT
          Interest Charges


Where TIE = Times Interest Earned
      EBIT = Earnings Before Interest and Taxes

                  BASED ON TABLE 6.2

TIE = 36,800     = 2.19
      16,800


TIE shows how many times the earnings of a firm will cover
its fixed interest expenses.  In Delta's case its income
available for meeting fixed interest costs will cover those
costs 2.19 times.
```

of bankruptcy that a jump in the company's cost of capital results, then the company has gone too far. When does that point occur? There are no fixed answers; a lot depends on how well the company can cover debt obligations, at least in the eyes of investors. For that reason it is necessary to look at the times interest earned. This ratio, the formula, and the calculation are shown in Table 6.3. A somewhat more sophisticated means of measuring debt utilizes income statement data. This involves the concept of financial leverage.

Financial Leverage

When a company utilizes debt financing, it increases its financial leverage. The concept of leverage is somewhat complex, because so many trade-offs are involved when a company relies on debt financing. On the one hand, debt means that a company can obtain productive facilities sooner than they might if they relied on internal sources of financing. Thus they may engage in return-generating activities that will have a positive effect on owner wealth. Not only that, but debt is a cheap form of financing. On the other hand, however, are the risks associated with debt financing. In other words, financial leverage can work for or against a company. It just depends on the economic circumstances.

To illustrate the concept of leverage, refer to Table 6.2, the 19X1 income statement for Delta Company. Notice that Delta has $16,800 worth of interest expense, which will have to be paid, regardless of whether Delta has a "good" year or a "bad" year. In other words, if Delta should generate sales of $2 million it would still only have to pay $16,800 of fixed interest expense, leaving the bulk of the added earnings for the benefit of shareholders. On the other hand, if Delta had $0 in sales, it would still have to cover the $16,800 in fixed interest expense. Obviously, that situation would work to the detriment of shareholders. To gauge the potential impact, Delta can calculate the "degree of financial leverage." The formula is

$$\text{DFL} = \frac{\% \, \Delta \text{ EPS or Net Income for Shareholders}}{\% \, \Delta \text{ EBIT}}$$

where DFL = Degree of Financial Leverage; EPS = Earnings Per Share; and EBIT = Earnings Before Interest and Taxes

To find the numbers to put into the equation, Delta should look at present activity from EBIT down to the bottom line. Then it should pick some other level of EBIT (at random; any other level will yield the correct results). Then Delta should calculate the bottom line at that level of EBIT. For an example refer to Table 6.4. Note that with a 10 percent level of increase in EBIT, Delta's bottom line would increase to $11,840, an increase of $1,840 over $10,000 ($1,840 is 18.4 percent of $10,000). In other words, if Delta's EBIT should increase only 10 percent, net income available for shareholders would increase 18.4 percent. Shareholders would probably be happy.

To calculate the degree of financial leverage, put the appropriate numbers into the formula as shown in the bottom of Table 6.4. Delta winds up with a degree of financial leverage of 1.84. This means for every percent of EBIT that Delta might anticipate, its percentage increase in net income available for shareholders should be 1.84 times that. In other words, if Delta anticipates a 20 percent increase in sales, its percentage increase in net income should be 1.84 times that, or 36.8 percent.

Table 6.4
Calculation of DFL, 10 Percent Increase

EBIT	$ 36,800	40,480
Interest	- 16,800	-16,800
EBT	20,000	23,680
Taxes (50%)	- 10,000	-11,840
Net Income	10,000	11,840

$$\text{DFL} = \frac{\% \, \Delta \text{ Net Income}}{\% \, \Delta \text{ EBIT}} = \frac{18.4}{10} = 1.84$$

What if EBIT went down? In that case financial leverage would work against the shareholders. For an example refer to Table 6.5. In this case it is obvious that although Delta's sales would go down only 10 percent, net income would decrease 18.4 percent. In that case, shareholders would probably be less than pleased.

A couple of points should be made regarding the degree of financial leverage. First of all, it applies only for planning purposes. Obviously, there are a number of variables that affect bottom-line outcome in actual business situations. In other words, the degree of financial leverage is only a guide to use in management decision making. The second point is that the degree of financial leverage applies only to the present level of output. Once a company actually moves to a new level of output, then a new degree of financial leverage applies.

To illustrate how the degree of financial leverage might be used as a guide to management decision making, refer to Table 6.6. This table shows the pro forma income statement for Delta Company that was formulated in Chapter 3. Remember that Delta decided to pay off a great deal of its debt. The calculation for the degree of financial leverage based on this pro forma statement appears in Table 6.7. Delta's degree of financial leverage based on this information is 1.13. That means that for every percentage increase in EBIT it might experience from that point, the change in net income would be 1.13 times that. In other words, if Delta's EBIT went up 20 percent, net income would go up only 22.6 percent. On the other hand, if Delta's sales went down 20 percent, net income would fall only 22.6 percent. What is the potential impact? Again, it depends on the circumstances. Suppose that Delta knows that a recession is looming, and that industry sales are probably going to take a sharp downward turn over the ensuing five-year period. In that case the proposed level of financing is

Table 6.5
Calculation of DFL, 10 Percent Decrease

EBIT	$ 36,800	33,120
Interest	– 16,800	–16,800
EBT	20,000	16,320
Taxes (50%)	– 10,000	–16,320
Net Income	10,000	8,160

$$DFL = \frac{\% \, \triangle \, \text{Net Income}}{\% \, \triangle \, \text{EBIT}} = \frac{-18.4}{-10} = 1.84$$

Table 6.6
Pro Forma Income Statement, Delta Company

Sales	$240,000
Cost of Goods Sold	140,750
Gross Profits	99,250
Selling & Administrative Costs	27,500
Earnings Before Interest & Taxes	71,750
Interest *	8,400
Earnings Before Taxes	63,350
Taxes **	31,675
NET INCOME	31,675

* Based on last year's interest cost. As Delta goes through the planning process, it may want to adjust this amount, should it decide to seek additional financing or pay off old debt.

** Assuming 50 percent taxes

Table 6.7
Calculation of DFL Pro Forma

EBIT	$ 71,750	78,925
Interest	- 8,400	- 8,400
EBT	63,350	70,525
Taxes (50%)	- 31,675	-35,262
Net Income	31,675	35,263

$$DFL = \frac{\% \triangle \text{Net Income}}{\% \triangle \text{EBIT}} = \frac{11.3}{10} = 1.13$$

probably appropriate. Although sales will go down and net income will also go down, net income will not be subject to the magnified effect that would result from a higher level of fixed debt financing.

If Delta predicts a rapidly expanding environment, however, shareholders would probably desire that a larger percentage of growth be financed with debt.

This would result in a favorable magnified effect on its net income as a result of any increase in EBIT. Another way of looking at impact on shareholders is to look at the result of increases of EBIT on earnings per share.

EBIT AND EPS

Because of the varying effects of financial leverage, it is helpful to depict graphically the effect of proposed financing plans in order to find the "financial breakeven point" of various financing plans. The best explanation of financial breakeven is an example.

Example

Assume that Alpha Company is seeking to obtain additional financing in the amount of $73,330. An investment banker has already been consulted and various financing packages have been formulated and discussed. After looking at the advantages and disadvantages of all the options, Alpha then looked at the factors outlined in this chapter such as control, legal implications, and the like. Eventually the company narrowed its options down to two different plans. Plan A relies more heavily on debt financing. It involves selling $20,000 worth of bonds at 10 percent. In addition, the company will sell 600 shares of $40 preferred stock that pays a 10 percent dividend. Assume in this case that the market value as well as the par value of the preferred stock is $40. The final detail of the plan is the sale of 1,000 shares of common stock at $29.33. Plan B involves selling $10,000 worth of 10 percent bonds, 300 shares of 10 percent preferred stock at $40, and 1,750 shares of common stock at $29.33. For purposes of expedience, Plan A might be called the debt plan and Plan B the equity plan. This terminology is obviously not entirely accurate. The company is in the 40 percent tax bracket. For convenience, Table 6.8 summarizes the particulars of the two plans.

The company has examined all relevant factors and decides that it is completely indifferent on all counts between the two plans. It then decides to find the

Table 6.8
Financing Plans

Plan A (Debt Plan)	
10% Bonds	$20,000
600 Shares 10% Preferred Stock ($40)	24,000
1000 Shares Common Stock @ $29.33	29,330
TOTAL	73,330
Plan B (Equity Plan)	
10% Bonds	$10,000
300 Shares 10% Preferred Stock ($40)	12,000
1750 Shares Common Stock @ $29.33	51,328
TOTAL	73,328

financial breakeven point. To find the financial breakeven point, it arbitrarily picks two different levels of EBIT, calculates EPS, and graphs the results. For example, starting with Plan A: The company picks two levels of EBIT arbitrarily. Assume these are $7,000 and $14,000. Next the company calculates EPS at these levels. With Plan A, at $7,000 EBIT, the company will have $2,000 of interest charges. This is calculated by taking 10 percent of the $20,000 worth of bonds to be sold under this plan. Taking the $2,000 interest from EBIT of $7,000 leaves the company with $5,000 of taxable income. Taxes will be 40 percent of this $5,000, or $2,000, leaving $3,000 after taxes. Next preferred dividends must be paid. These preferred dividends are 10 percent of the number of shares (600) times the par value ($40). The result is $2,400. This leaves $600 worth of earnings available for common shareholders. There are 1,000 shares of common stock, so EPS are $.60 ($600/1,000). These calculations and those for the $14,000 level are shown in Table 6.9.

Now the company should perform the same procedure for Plan B. Results are illustrated in Table 6.10.

Table 6.9
EBIT-EPS Calculations, Plan A

EBIT	7,000	14,000
INT	-2,000	- 2,000
EBT	5,000	12,000
TAXES	-2,000	- 4,800
EAT	3,000	7,200
PD	-2,400	- 2,400
EAC	600	4,800
SHARES	1,000	1,000
EPS	.60	4.80

EBIT	=	Earnings Before Interest and Taxes
INT	=	Interest
EBT	=	Earnings Before Taxes
EAT	=	Earnings After Taxes
PD	=	Preferred Dividends
EAC	=	Earnings available for Common Shareholders
SHARES	=	# of Shares of Common Stock
EPS	=	Earnings per Share

Table 6.10
EBIT-EPS Calculations, Plan B

EBIT	7,000	14,000
INT	-1,000	-1,000
EBT	6,000	13,000
TAXES	-2,400	-5,200
EAT	3,600	7,800
PD	-1,200	-1,200
EAC	2,400	6,600
SHARES	1,750	1,750
EPS	1.37	3.77

Next the company graphs the results. Plan A involves plotting two points: $.60 EPS $7,000 EBIT and $4.80 EPS $14,000 EBIT. Plan B's points are $1.37 EPS $7,000 EBIT, and $3.77 EPS $14,000. See Figure 6.1 for an illustration.

Next the company draws a straight line through both points of each plan. The point of indifference is the point where the lines cross. Figure 6.2 shows this point. The point of indifference shows where shareholders would be indifferent (as far as EPS are concerned) as to which financing plan the company should choose to adopt. This point looks to be $10,000 EBIT. Table 6.11 confirms this. The point of indifference might be thought of as the financial breakeven point. This would be the point of EBIT that gives shareholders the same EPS under either plan. As seen in Table 6.11, at $10,000 shareholders get $2.40, regardless of whether the company chooses Plan A or Plan B. If the company's predicted EBIT over some relevant time horizon is going to be less than $10,000, then, all other things being equal, stockholders would prefer Plan B. If predicted EBIT were to be greater than $10,000, then shareholders would prefer Plan A.

Tables 6.12–6.15 and Figures 6.3–6.4 show another example of calculating the financial breakeven point. Note in this case as in the previous example that the debt plans are favored at higher levels of EBIT, and the equity plans are favored at lower levels. This is generally true, because of the effects of financial leverage already discussed. So the means of financing future growth will be quite important to shareholders. This brings to mind the implications of growth on planning. Chapter 7 covers growth considerations in detail.

Figure 6.1
Plotting of Points

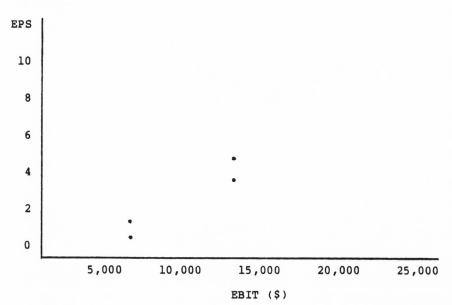

Figure 6.2
Point of Indifference

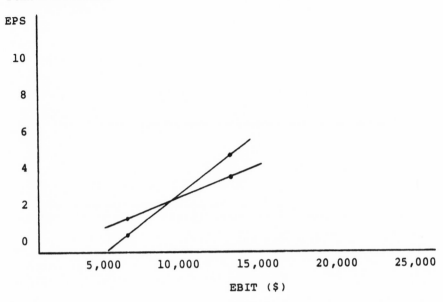

Table 6.11
Financial Breakeven

	PLAN A	PLAN B
EBIT	$10,000	$10,000
INT	-2,000	-1,000
EBT	8,000	9,000
TAXES	-3,200	-3,600
EAT	4,800	5,400
PD	-2,400	-1,200
EAC	2,400	4,200
SHARES	1,000	1,750
EPS	$2.40	$2.40

Table 6.12
Financing Plan

PLAN A (DEBT PLAN)

    6% Bonds $700,000

    20,000 Shares 7% Preferred ($10)   200,000

    10,000 Shares of Common @ $10   100,000

        TOTAL $1,000,000

PLAN B (EQUITY PLAN)

    6% Bonds $400,000

    10,000 Shares 7% Preferred ($10)   100,000

    50,000 Shares of Common @ $10   500,000

        TOTAL $1,000,000

Company is in 15% tax bracket.

Table 6.13
EBIT-EPS Calculations, Plan A

EBIT	$60,000	$150,000
INT	− 42,000	− 42,000
EBT	18,000	108,000
TAXES	− 2,700	− 16,200
EAT	15,300	91,800
PD	− 14,000	− 14,000
EAC	1,300	77,800
SHARES	10,000	10,000
EPS	$.13	$7.78

Table 6.14
EBIT-EPS Calculations, Plan B

EBIT	$60,000	$150,000
INT	− 24,000	− 24,000
EBT	36,000	126,000
TAXES	− 5,400	− 18,900
EAT	30,600	107,100
PD	− 7,000	− 7,000
EAC	23,600	100,100
SHARES	50,000	50,000
EPS	$.47	$2.00

Table 6.15
Financial Breakeven

	PLAN A	PLAN B
EBIT	$65,000	$65,000
INT	−42,000	−24,000
EBT	23,000	41,000
TAXES	− 3,450	− 6,150
EAT	19,550	34,850
PD	−14,000	− 7,000
EAC	5,550	27,850
SHARES	10,000	50,000
EPS	$.56	$.56

Figure 6.3
Plotting of Points

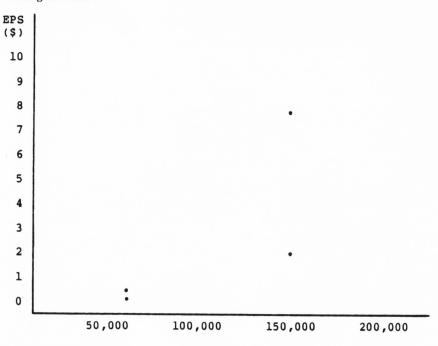

Figure 6.4
Point of Indifference

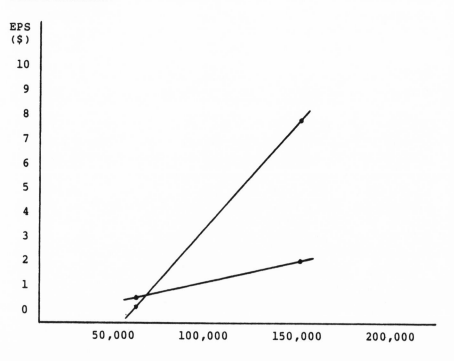

7

FORECASTING GROWTH

Growth is a necessary part of a capitalistic system. Growth at the firm level is valued very highly by the securities markets. On the other hand, growth can create many problems for a company, not the least of which is an insatiable need for funds. Growth can be orderly and restrained, or it can be unrestrained. The difference between restrained and unrestrained growth is more than a matter of magnitude. The difference depends primarily on how well the company has planned for its growth. Proper planning for growth means that the company has planned for all of its resource needs, both production and financial.

Business history contains many examples of companies that have grown in an unrestrained manner and that subsequently faced severe financial difficulties. Peoples Express, the reduced-rate airline, is one such example, but the classic case of a company that did not survive its growth is Sambo's, the restaurant chain.

Sambo's revenues grew at a compound rate of 42.7 percent per year between 1973 and 1979. Typically speaking, a company cannot grow at this pace without either raising new equity capital through a stock sale or by increasing its debt ratios substantially. Sambo's was no exception. Its debt to equity ratio grew from a very modest 36 percent in 1973 to 312 percent in 1979. Sambo's filed for bankruptcy in early 1982. Perfect hindsight shows that Sambo's grew too quickly, with dire consequences. Proper planning could have prevented its demise. One way to look at the issue of company growth is to think in terms of the "three M's."

THE THREE M'S

Marketing, management, and money: three building blocks of a successful company. It is obvious that no company can grow without having the three M's going for it.

Marketing: In order to grow, a company has to sell its product and has to expand its market.

Management: The management of a company has to grow as the company grows, not so much in terms of numbers of personnel, but in terms of ideas.

Money: If a company grows, its need for resources will grow, necessitating additional funds.

The problem with the three M's is that the growth in each of the three areas should be orderly, uniform, and well-planned, as illustrated in Figure 7.1.

Figure 7.1
Orderly Growth

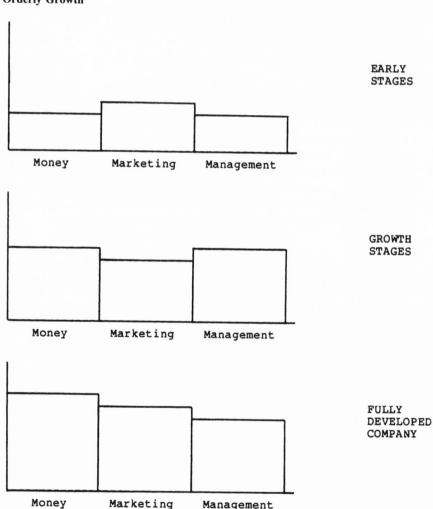

If this pattern is not followed, however, companies can get in trouble. Figure 7.2 shows a company destined for trouble. A company whose sales are growing quickly may mistakenly think everything is rosy. Sales are going up like crazy, the company is making money hand over fist, and the end appears nowhere in sight. In the background, however, potential problems are festering. If sales are growing like crazy, eventually additional resources will be required. If the company has no rational plan for obtaining these additional resources, it may reach a point where it is operating at full capacity but the lead time for expansion is too far away. The company must turn away sales, and the competition will certainly step in to take up the slack. By the time the company has expanded, it may have lost all its market.

Figure 7.3 illustrates a situation that is not uncommon. The management of the company has dreams that far outstrip the resources of the company. A fancy new plant is built, a lot of consultants are employed, innovative investing schemes are undertaken, and the like. The problem is that the company jumped the gun. It had neither the financial wherewithal nor the sales and profits to back up its dreams. Rather than take a measured attitude toward growth, the company let its dreams run away with its future.

Sometimes a company doesn't dream big enough. Figure 7.4 illustrates a situation where the company has financial resources at its disposal, but doesn't

Figure 7.2
Rapid Sales Growth

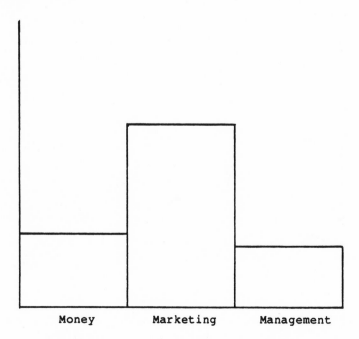

Money   Marketing   Management

Figure 7.3
Rapid Resource Growth

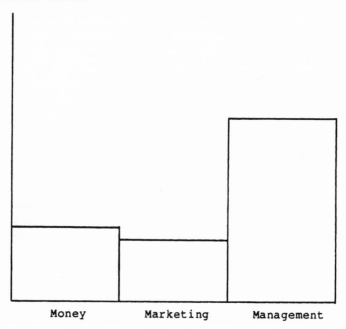

Figure 7.4
Idle Cash

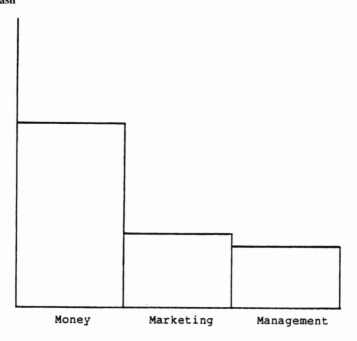

utilize them effectively. It should be investing in return-generating resources—the building blocks of the future. As with all other aspects of a business, a company should have an effective plan for obtaining and managing growth. The rest of this chapter will allow an analyst to determine when a company has grown in an unrestrained manner, and will show how to determine the pace at which a company can safely grow.

UNRESTRAINED GROWTH

How can someone determine when a company has grown too quickly? The answer is found by computing two simple financial ratios. The first is the fixed asset to net worth ratio, and the second is the net sales to net worth or trading ratio. When either of these ratios becomes large relative to the industry average for this ratio or relative to the company's own historical average for this ratio, then unrestrained growth has occurred.

The two ratios are examined individually. When a company's fixed assets increase over time, the company may finance the increase with net worth, long-term debt, short-term debt, and/or a reduction in current assets. If some proportion of net worth is not used in the financing plan, then the funds for the fixed assets have come from long-term debt, short-term debt, or current assets. The result is that the company's liquidity has been reduced and/or debt usage has increased. It is very likely that the managers of the company did not decide to create liquidity or debt problems. Instead, they decided to buy the fixed assets, but the result was that debt and/or liquidity problems followed.

When the ratio of fixed assets to net worth rises, it shows that the increase in fixed assets was financed with proportionately more debt or working capital than with net worth. In situations like this, unrestrained growth has occurred. The result of an increase in the fixed asset to net worth ratio will always be a reduction in liquidity or an increase in debt usage. However, profitability may also suffer. Fixed assets must typically be insured and most states have business property taxes that must be paid. In addition, increased interest costs from the debt financing will further impair profitability. Unrestrained growth of fixed assets can cause a company considerable problems.

The second ratio, net sales to net worth, commonly called the trading ratio, also shows when a company has grown too fast. When sales rise, as demonstrated in Chapter 4, a company must increase its assets. If these assets are financed with increases in current or long-term debt (instead of net worth), then the trading ratio will get large. This type of company is an overtrader. Overtraders are usually characterized by inadequate liquidity and excessive debt. Very rapid sales growth with insufficient equity financing causes overtrading, which in extreme cases will bankrupt a company.

Sambo's ratios illustrate these points. In 1974 its fixed asset to net worth ratio and trading ratio were 94 percent and 1.95, respectively. By 1979 these growth measures had increased to 1001 percent and 15.64. Sambo's was clearly an overtrader. Could Sambo's have done anything to prevent its demise? The answer is yes. By planning its growth and even perhaps limiting (not eliminating) its growth Sambo's could have stayed in business. Its rapidly increasing revenues demonstrated an acceptance of its product, and this is half the battle. The other half is planning, which Sambo's apparently did not do. If Sambo's had limited its growth to a sustainable rate, its financial ratios would not have deteriorated. In the next section, the maximum rate at which a firm can grow will be computed. The consequences of growing faster than this maximum rate will also be discussed.

MAXIMUM SUSTAINABLE GROWTH

The basic percent of sales model was presented in Chapter 4; it will be used to develop the maximum sustainable growth rate. The model can be presented as:

$$EFR = SA/S \; \Delta \; S + \Delta \; FA - SL/S \; \Delta \; S - (S + \Delta \; S)(PM)(1 - PO)$$

The various terms are the same as in Chapter 4.

There are two basic assumptions in developing this idea: (1) the firm has some target debt to asset ratio, and (2) has limited ability or desire to input additional equity capital. These assumptions are not unrealistic. Most companies attempt to limit debt usage to a specific level, perhaps an industry average. In other cases, these companies may have a limit placed upon them by their lending institution. When a company borrows money from a bank or other lending institution, the financial managers must agree to very specifically defined covenants. One of the most common restrictions is a limit on future debt usage. Typically speaking, companies find that raising new equity is difficult. The existing owners may not have the personal wealth to continue to supply the firm with capital. Finding new partners may also be difficult, and many owners may not want to share authority and income. Thus while limited new equity is one of the model's assumptions, the model will be general enough to include new externally generated equity for those situations in which it is available.

DEVELOPING THE MODEL

The constraining factor to the firm in a growth situation is the lack of external equity and the target debt to asset ratio. We must first develop an expression for the debt to asset ratio on the new assets, which can be represented as follows:

$$D/A = \frac{(EFR - EE) + (SL/S) \; (\Delta \; S)}{(SA/S) \; (S) + FA}$$

The numerator shows the new debt that can be added. The first term is the EFR less any external equity. This difference would be the portion of the EFR financed with debt. The second term is the new spontaneous liabilities. These would have to be considered part of the new debt. In the denominator, the new spontaneous assets and new fixed assets are included. The expression therefore shows the new debt divided by the new assets. The size of the debt to asset ratio will limit the amount of sales growth. If the expression from the basic percent of sales method for EFR is substituted into the debt to asset ratio shown above, and ΔS is solved for, the maximum sustainable growth model results:

$$\Delta S = \frac{(FA)\,(1 - D/A) - (S)\,(PM)\,(1 - D) - EE}{(SA/S)\,(D/A - 1) + (PM)\,(1 - D)}$$

By substituting the financial data for a company into the sustainable growth equation, a company might see how fast it can grow, assuming that new equity is limited and that the company has a desire to limit debt growth. Growing faster than the specified rate implies that (1) new equity can be acquired and/or (2) the firm relaxes its debt to asset constraint.

USING THE MODEL

By substituting the appropriate information into the maximum sustainable growth model equation, the maximum rate at which the firm can grow is computed. An example of the computation appears in Table 7.1. In Panel A of the exhibit, a historical balance sheet appears for the Delta-Beta Company. The company wants to maintain its existing 43.2 percent debt to asset ratio. In order for a sales increase to occur, the company must increase its fixed assets by $2,000. In Panel B the computation of maximum sustainable growth is shown. Substituting the relevant data for the Delta-Beta Company into the equation, it is apparent that a growth in sales of $5,811 is possible. On a percentage basis, this is a growth rate of 5.81 percent ($5,811/$100,000).

What would happen if fixed assets were to grow by, say, $12,000? Substituting the relevant data into the equation reveals ΔS of ($10,381). A negative ΔS implies that, given the constraints on debt and no available externally generated equity, positive growth is impossible. New growth could occur only if the debt to asset constraint is relaxed, a situation that can lead to overtrading.

What if new equity is available? When new external equity is available, then a larger sales increase is possible. For the Delta-Beta Company, each $1.00 of new equity permits sales to increase by $2.72. So an increase in equity of $1,000 would allow sales to go up by $2,720. The increased equity permits the acquisition of new assets financed by the equity and permits additional debt to be added without violating the debt to asset constraint.

A second general observation can be made. Depreciation is similar to a source of funds. When depreciation amounts are to be charged against net income, and no new fixed assets are required, Δ FA is negative. Δ FA was defined as the change to net fixed assets—new fixed assets less depreciation. A negative Δ FA reduces EFR. Thus depreciation serves to reduce the EFR even if FA is positive because it is subtracted from the new fixed assets.

Table 7.1
Delta-Beta Company 19X5 Balance Sheet

PANEL A

Cash	$ 10,000	Accounts Payable .	$ 5,000
Marketable		Accruals	2,000
Securities ...	5,000	Notes Payable	
Receivables	25,000	at 10%	12,000
Inventory	35,000		
		Total	$ 19,000
Total	$ 75,000		
		Long-Term Debt	
		at 15%	48,000
Net Fixed Assets .	80,000	Common Stock	32,000
		Retained Earnings	56,000
Total Assets	$155,000	Total	$155,000

OTHER SELECTED DATA

19X5 Sales	$100,000
19X5 Net Income	5,000
19X5 Dividends	$ 2,000

EXAMPLE

Assume that Delta-Beta Company wants to keep its existing
debt to asset ratio. What is the maximum Δ S that it can
achieve given the information above?

Delta-Beta's existing debt to asset ratio is 43.2%.

PANEL B

$$\Delta S = \frac{\Delta FA(1-D/A) - S(P.M.)(1-P.O.)}{\frac{SA}{S}(D/A-1) + P.M.(1-P.O.)}$$

$$\Delta S = \frac{2000(1-.432) - (100,000)(.05)(1-.4)}{.7(.432-1) + (.05)(1-.4)}$$

$$\Delta S = 5070$$

VIOLATING THE MAXIMUM SUSTAINABLE GROWTH

What happens when a company violates its maximum sustainable growth? Sambo's presents an interesting case. In Table 7.2 the financial statements for Sambo's are summarized and the percentage of maximum sustainable growth is computed. The percentage of sustainable growth for 1975 is computed from 1974 data, except that the actual increase in fixed assets in 1975 over 1974 is used for Δ FA.

In 1975 Sambo's sold common stock. By raising external equity, it had a sustainable growth rate of 165.1 percent. Sambo's actually grew by only 37.7 percent in 1975. Notice that since actual growth exceeded sustainable growth Sambo's debt to asset ratio dropped from 28.6 to 25.4 percent.

In 1976 Sambo's acquired a considerable amount of fixed assets. Its sales increased by 173.7 percent. Given the large increase in fixed assets, the lack of externally generated equity, and the modest debt to asset constraint, Sambo's could not afford this much sales growth. Its sustainable growth rate was negative. Since growth occurred, the debt to asset ratio grew to 34.6 percent.

Table 7.2
Sambo's Actual Sales Growth versus Sustainable Growth

	1974	1975	1976	1977
Revenues	$100,872	$138,944	$380,318	$491,753
Income	12,846	17,641	23,066	22,771
Dividends	1,169	1,922	4,109	10,482
Current Assets	20,509	28,880	49,021	80,482
Non-Current Assets	51,951	82,821	106,917	301,068
Debt/Assets	28.6%	25.4%	34.6%	70.0%
External Equity	-	15,872	-	-
Actual Growth Rate	-	37.7%	173.7%	29.3%
Sustainable Growth Rate*		165.1%	(38.9%)	(641.6%)

* The sustainable growth rate for 1975 uses the actual change in
  fixed assets from 1974 to 1975 and uses 1974 data for other
  variables. The sustainable growth rate for 1976 is based on
  1975 data etc.

In 1977 noncurrent assets nearly tripled. With no available external equity, Sambo's could not sustain this growth. Nevertheless, sales growth occurred. The result was a more than doubling in the debt to asset ratio, from 34.6 to 70.0 percent. When growth occurs at a rapid rate, a company must either raise equity or be willing to accept an increased debt ratio. The only other solution is to limit growth.

CONCLUSIONS

It is of utmost importance for a company to plan its future. Among the factors for which a company should plan are growth in sales and resources. A managed growth pattern should be the objective of the planner. The sustainable growth rate for a company can be computed. This is an intregal part of the forecasting process. When combined with the basic forecasting model found in Chapter 4 it allows a firm to plan for the future.

___ 8 ___

AN ADVANCED FORECASTING MODEL

This chapter refines the basic shortcut model and allows more sophisticated forecasting. It reviews some basic statistical procedures and as such may not be of much interest to any but the more ambitious of readers. Regression analysis, which is the basis of this chapter, is routinely performed by many a software program and is therefore of little concern to managers. However, any reader who is interested in what the programs are doing will find this chapter helpful.

In this chapter statistical procedures in forecasting the balance sheet are reviewed. The procedures as outlined can be quite easily mastered, and, in fact, many calculators (priced under $50) will perform these statistical procedures. The procedure used is called regression analysis. It illustrates how one variable changes when another variable changes. For example, regression analysis might be used to predict how a change in sales affects the spontaneous accounts on the balance sheet. In the basic shortcut chapter the assumption was made that the relationship between sales and the spontaneous accounts could be defined by a simple percentage. Regression analysis is a more exact way to relate these variables.

The first section of the chapter is a review of the basic model. Then regression analysis will be explained in general terms. Finally, regression is used to forecast. Along the way, regression is calculated by hand, which is quite frankly a time-consuming (and painful) process.

A REVIEW OF THE BASIC MODEL

Chapter 4 covered the percent of sales model. This model presumes that a constant percentage relationship exists between sales and the spontaneous accounts. If, for example, accounts receivable is 18 percent of sales, the model presumes that this 18 percent remains constant despite any changes in sales. This assumption, as it turns out, is fine for very modest variations in sales; but when sales are expected to go up or down by relatively large amounts, this assumption may no longer be valid, and it may lead to inaccurate forecasts.

Figure 8.1 depicts the relationship between sales and the spontaneous accounts. The relationship is linear and starts at the origin (the point on the graph where sales and the spontaneous accounts are both zero). In a situation in which sales are expected to change by, say, 4 or 5 percent, then the percent of sales model will probably work as well as other models. Regression analysis allows a relationship that is not quite as limiting as in the percent of sales method. The regression analysis procedure is discussed in the next section.

REGRESSION ANALYSIS

Regression analysis is a general statistical technique through which the analyst can determine a linear relationship between a dependent variable (the spontaneous accounts) and one or more independent or predictor variables (sales). The technique can be used to describe a relationship or to predict. This chapter explores its use for its predictive capabilities. Suppose, for example, that someone wanted

Figure 8.1
Percent of Sales Relationship

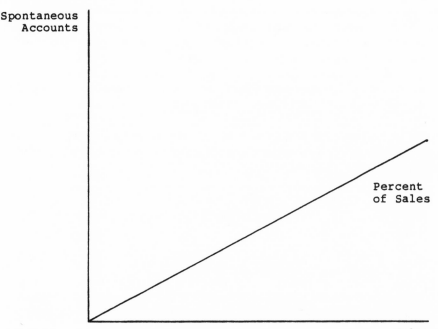

to determine how one of the spontaneous accounts changes when sales change. Through regression analysis we could obtain an equation that indicates what the statistical relationship between the two accounts is.

An equation for a straight line can be represented by the following expression:

$$y = a + bx$$

In this equation, the term y is the dependent variable. This means that y depends upon the other variable, x. The term x is the independent variable. The two symbols, a and b, represent regression parameters. The intercept of a line is represented by a, and the slope by b. This line is shown in Figure 8.2. The intercept of a line is the point at which the line crosses the y axis. The slope of a line is the rate at which the line rises. Simple algebra dictates that the slope of a line is the rate at which the line rises over the rate at which the line runs horizontally. The slope is often defined as the rise over the run.

Figure 8.2 shows a straight line. The dependent variable is the variable to be predicted, the spontaneous accounts. The independent variable is sales. In other

Figure 8.2
Regression Analysis

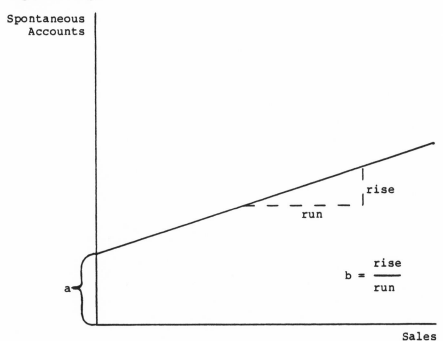

words, the spontaneous accounts depend upon sales, which is the same assumption made in the percent of sales method. Regression analysis yields the equation:

Y	=	a	+	bx
Spontaneous	=	slope	+	(slope) (sales)
Accounts				

The logic behind a regression analysis is based upon a scatter diagram, an example of which appears in Figure 8.3. On a graph, the points that depict values for a spontaneous account and sales would be plotted. For example, if there are ten years worth of information, the value for sales and the spontaneous account for year one, the values for year two, year three, and so on would be plotted. On the graph, there would be ten points. A line is then placed to minimize the distance between the points and the line. This line is called the line of "best fit." If regression is done visually, as suggested above, there is considerable room for error. Finding the "best line" may depend upon who is attempting to fit the line between the points.

Figure 8.3
Scatterplot

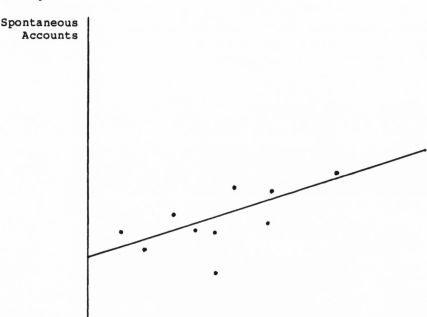

Spontaneous
Accounts

Sales

The statistical procedure of regression analysis fits the line. Technically, it finds the line that minimizes the square of the distance between the line and the points. This form of regression is often called "Least Square" or "Ordinary Least Square" regression. So far the regression procedure has been discussed only in general terms. In the next section the regression equation is computed. One final note is important, however. Since it is necessary to know what the separate relationship is between each of the spontaneous accounts and sales, a completely different regression must be conducted for each spontaneous account. It is necessary to run one regression between sales and cash, one between sales and receivables, one between sales and each of the other spontaneous accounts.

REGRESSION COMPUTATIONS

The variable y was previously defined to be the dependent variable and x to be the independent variable. These correspond to the spontaneous accounts and sales, respectively. The spontaneous accounts are said to be the dependent variable because they depend on sales. Sales is the independent variable because it is determined by customer behavior, which is independent of the spontaneous accounts. In this section, equations with x and y are shown because the equations will be long enough without writing out the words, sales and spontaneous accounts, each time.

Figure 8.4 shows the equation for the computation of the slope and the intercept of the regression equation. The procedure for computing these numbers by hand will be summarized below. However, it is not recommended that anyone try to

Figure 8.4
Manual Regression Computation

To compute the slope:

$$b = \frac{\sum_{i=1}^{N} (x_i - \bar{x})(y_i - \bar{y})}{\sum_i (x_i - \bar{x})^2}$$

To compute the intercept:

$$a = \bar{y} - b\bar{x}$$

Where:

x_i = each observation of the independent variable

$\bar{x}$ = average of the independent variables

y_i = each observation of the dependent variable

$\bar{y}$ = average of the dependent variable

compute regression equations by hand. It is a long and time-consuming procedure. The following computations are presented simply to illustrate regression computations.

First, the x and the y variables must be averaged. These averages are called x and y. Then, as shown in the figure, the average of the x variables is subtracted from each x variable and is multiplied by the corresponding computation for the y values. These are then summed. Finally, the difference between each x value and the average is squared. These are summed and divided into the previously summed value. This produces the slope, b. The intercept is computed by substituting the b value obtained above into an equation with the average x and y values. The regression equation is obtained.

An example of this computation appears in Table 8.1. In this table seven years of financial data for sales and cash appear. These are the x and y variables, respectively, and are the values to be used in the computation. Column 1 shows the year; columns 2 and 3 show the cash and sales values for each year, and the averages are shown at the bottom. In column 4 each x value and each y value is reduced by its respective average. Finally, the square of the difference between the average of the sales values and the sales values is shown in column 5.

The slope of the line, b, is .0674. This implies that if sales increase by, say, $100, that cash would increase by 6.74 percent, or $6.74. The intercept of the line is $ - 2,635. The fact that this number is negative does not hurt the analysis.

The resulting equation that relates cash and sales is:

$$\text{Cash} = -2,635 + (.0674)(\text{sales})$$

This line can be used to predict future cash amounts and to be part of the computation required for preparing a pro forma balance sheet. In the next section, the predictive uses of the equation are discussed.

PREDICTING WITH REGRESSION ANALYSIS

In the previous section a regression equation was developed for cash and sales. Suppose that sales are forecast to be $380,600 in 1987. The regression equation can be used to predict the probable cash balance of the company.

$$\text{Cash} = -2,635 + (.0674)(380,600)$$
$$= \$23,017$$

This procedure would then be repeated for each of the spontaneous accounts. Estimates for the regression statistics for each spontaneous account would have to be obtained to compute the values of each spontaneous account. If it were done by hand, the odds of making an error or two would be substantial, not to mention the fact that a large amount of time would be wasted punching buttons on a calculator. It is much easier to perform a regression analysis on a calculator that is made to do regressions or, obviously, with the aid of a computer.

Table 8.1
Regression Computation Example

1	2	3	4	5
Year	Y Cash	X Sales	$(X_i-\bar{X})$ $(Y-\bar{Y})$	$(X_i-\bar{X})2$
1980	10,200	180,000	275,095,359	4,804,014,721
1981	11,000	200,000	156,266,559	2,431,574,721
1982	11,500	220,000	78,231,059	859,134,721
1983	12,100	233,400	32,919,859	253,159,921
1984	17,400	280,200	99,802,359	954,130,321
1985	19,500	327,100	414,693,160	6,051,128,521
1986	17,480	304,480	182,664,560	3,043,618,561
Sum	99,180	1,745,180	1,239,672,915	18,396,761,490
Average	14,169	249,311		

To compute the slope

$$b = \frac{1,239,672,915}{18,396,761,490} = .0674$$

To compute the intercept

$$a = 14,169 - (.0674) \times (249,311) = -2635$$

Regression Equation

$$Cash = -2635 + (.0674) (Sales)$$

REGRESSION WITH A CALCULATOR

Today, inexpensive calculators can be purchased that compute the regression statistics. The procedure, which would normally take an hour or two if done by hand, can be completed in a very few minutes with a calculator. Figure 8.5 shows the computations for the Texas Instruments BA–55 calculator. A different calculator would require different steps, but essentially they work the same. One would simply input the data points, being sure to input the dependent and independent variables in the correct order. The calculator is then instructed to to compute the intercept and slope (and the correlation coefficient discussed below).

Figure 8.5
Regression Computation on a Texas Instruments - BA–55 Calculator

180,000	X/Y	10,200	Σ +
200,000	X/Y	11,000	Σ +
220,000	X/Y	11,500	Σ +
233,400	X/Y	12,100	Σ +
280,200	X/Y	17,400	Σ +
327,100	X/Y	19,500	Σ +
304,480	X/Y	17,480	Σ +

Display

To compute a	2nd	Intcp	-2635
To compute b	2nd	Slope	.0674
To compute R	2nd	Corr	.959

CORRELATION COEFFICIENT

The correlation coefficient is another statistic that a calculator can provide. This number will tell how strong the relationship between sales and the spontaneous accounts is. In other words, it lets someone know how reliable the regression equation is for forecasting purposes. The correlation coefficient is a single number that can be computed and it provides the analyst with useful information. The correlation coefficient, R, can vary from − 1 to + 1. R tells the extent to which variables are related. If R is positive, then the variables are positively related. Thus, an increase in sales would be associated with an increase in cash. If R is negative, just the opposite is true. An increase in sales would be associated with a decrease in cash.

The closer that R is to 1, the more highly correlated the two variables are. Thus, an R of, say, .89 would mean that sales and a particular spontaneous account such as cash are very closely related. An R of only .12 would mean that the variables are not closely related, and forecasts based on such data will likely be subject to more error.

The formula for computing the correlation coefficient, R, is shown in Figure 8.5. This is another very tedious and time-consuming computation. A calculator can usually provide results in less than half the time that it would take to compute the data manually.

OVERALL EXAMPLE

In Table 8.2, a set of financial information has been presented for the Public Company. Comparative data from Omega Company are also included. This information will be used to prepare a pro forma balance sheet for 1987, using the 1980 through 1986 financial reports. The example assumes that sales are expected to increase by 25 percent in 1987 over 1986 sales. In addition, fixed assets are expected to increase by $18,000, and $10,000 of long-term debt will

Table 8.2
Public Company Selected Income Figures

	1980	1981	1982	1983	1984	1985	1986
Net Sales	180,000	200,000	220,000	233,400	280,000	327,100	304,480
Gross Profit	71,300	74,500	79,200	83,970	95,290	111,999	107,840
Earnings before	interest						
and taxes	24,000	26,000	9,500	29,930	33,300	40,550	34,850
Interest	1,500	1,200	1,240	1,230	2,100	4,730	6,600
Net Income	12,330	13,566	4,492	15,230	15,660	17,080	13,390
Dividend	4,930	5,426	3,560	6,070	7,860	7,330	8,080

OMEGA COMPANY

COMPARATIVE BALANCE SHEET

Assets

Cash	10,200	11,000	11,500	12,100	17,400	19,500	17,480
Receivables	25,300	27,000	30,000	31,400	35,600	46,500	53,700
Inventories	57,200	60,000	60,500	64,700	79,000	100,800	97,320
Total Current							
Assets	92,700	98,000	102,000	108,200	132,000	166,800	168,500
Net Plant	47,000	46,000	45,000	46,200	58,600	68,900	72,020
Misc. Assets	10,700	10,700	10,700	10,700	11,900	12,700	15,440
Total Assets	150,400	154,700	157,700	165,100	202,500	248,400	255,960

Liabilities and Capital

Accounts Payable	7,000	8,000	9,000	7,000	15,200	24,600	24,530
Other Current							
Liabilities	20,000	21,000	22,000	23,500	26,900	35,000	36,750
Total Current							
Liabilities	27,000	29,000	31,000	30,500	42,100	59,600	61,280
Long-term Debt	15,000	12,000	12,400	12,400	28,700	45,700	46,040
Deferred Taxes	2,300	2,400	2,500	2,570	4,580	5,380	7,140
Other Liabilities	1,600	1,500	1,500	2,030	1,520	2,570	1,050
Total							
Liabilities	45,900	44,900	47,400	47,500	76,900	113,250	115,510
Net Worth*	104,500	109,800	110,300	117,600	125,600	135,150	140,450
Total	150,400	154,700	157,700	165,100	202,500	248,400	255,906

* The company maintains an Employee Stock Plan. Periodically the company sells small amounts of stock to employees and repurchases it when they retire.

Assume: (1) 25% sales increase in 1987 is expected over 1986 sales: 1987 sales are expected to be $380,600.
(2) A Fixed Asset Increase of $18,000 is necessary.
(3) $10,000 principal of long-term debt is due.

be retired. These nonspontaneous accounts are treated the same as in the percent of sales procedure. The expected changes to the nonspontaneous accounts are added to the balances.

Separate regressions are computed for cash, receivables, inventory, accounts payable, other current liabilities, and net income. These regressions, as shown in Table 8.3, are used to forecast 1987 balances. The R statistics are all strong, except the one for net income. In spite of the weak R for net income, these regressions will be used to obtain the balance sheet.

At the bottom of Table 8.3, the balances for the spontaneous accounts are computed using the regression equations. These are put together to obtain the pro forma balance sheet, shown in Table 8.4. Fixed assets are increased by the forecasted amount, $18,000, and long-term debt is reduced by $10,000. The total assets sum to $288,135, while the liabilities and net worth sum to only $264,112. The difference is the EFR, $24,023. The EFR is interpreted in the

Table 8.3
Regression Results

	Intercept		Slope		R
Spontaneous Assets					
Cash =	-2,635	+	.0674	sales	95.9%
Receivables =	-7,961	+	.1749	sales	83.2%
Inventory =	-6,061	+	.3220	sales	93.8%
Spontaneous Liabilities					
Accounts Payable =	-20,013	+	.1349	sales	87.5%
Other Current Liabilities =	-2,545	+	.1163	sales	89.2%
Other					
Net Income =	2,711	+	.0417	sales	22.8%

1987 Forecast

1. 25% sales increase over 1986 - expected sales: $380,600.

2. Fixed assets increase of 18,000 will be required.

3. $10,000 principal of long-term debt is due.

Forecast Results

Forecast Equations								Balances
Cash	=	-2635	+	(.0674)	X	(380,600)	=	23,017
Receivables	=	-7961	+	(.1749)	X	(380,600)	=	58,606
Inventory	=	-6061	+	(.3220)	X	(380,600)	=	116,492
Payable	=	-20,013	+	(.1349)	X	(380,600)	=	31,330
Other Liabilities	=	-2545	+	(.1163)	X	(380,600)	=	41,719
Net Income	=	2711	+	(.0417)	X	(380,600)	=	18,582

Table 8.4
Public Company 1987 Pro Forma Balance Sheet

Assets		Liabilities & Equity	
Cash	$ 23,017	Payables	$ 31,330
Receivables	58,606	Other	41,719
Inventory	$116,492	Total	73,049
Current Assets	198,115	Long-term debt	36,040
Net Plant	90,020	Deferred Taxes	7,140
Total Assets	$288,135	Net Worth*	147,883
		Subtotal	264,112
		EFR	24,023
		Total	$288,135

* 1987 Net Worth = 140,450 + (1 - .6) (18,582) = $147,883

same way as it was with the percent of sales. It is the amount of outside funding required if the company wants to maintain its financial condition and have the sales growth.

MAXIMUM SUSTAINABLE GROWTH WITH REGRESSION

In Chapter 7 the method by which the maximum sustainable growth of a company could be determined from the percent of sales method was discussed. It can be computed using regression, as well. For this computation, only three regressions are run: sales with total spontaneous assets, sales with total spontaneous liabilities, and sales with net income.

These regressions would take the form:

Spontaneous Assets	$SA = a_1 + b_1 (S + \Delta S)$
Spontaneous Liabilities	$SL = a_2 + b_2 (S + \Delta S)$
Net Income	$NI = a_3 + b_3 (S + \Delta S)$

After these three regressions have been computed, the maximum growth rate in sales becomes:

$$\Delta S = \Delta FA (1 - D/A) - (1 - PO) (a_3 + b_3 \Delta S) - EE\, b_1 (D/A - 1) + b_3 (1 - PO)$$

There is not too much difference between this expression and the one in Chapter 7. In this one, the regression slopes have replaced the simple percentages that were used with the percent of sales technique.

MULTIPLE REGRESSIONS

Simple regression uses only one independent variable. For this analysis, sales was the independent variable that determined the dependent variables, the spontaneous accounts. Multiple regression allows the use of more than one independent variable. For example, cash balances might depend upon several things, only one of which is sales. Cash may also depend on the level of interest rates in the economy, the availability of investments, and/or the season of the year. The resulting equation would look something like:

$$\text{Cash} = a + b_1 \text{ sales} + b_2 \text{ rates} + b_3 \text{ investment} + b_4 \text{ season} + \ldots$$

The statistical technique to determine this relationship is called multiple regression. To use this technique requires statistical programs, which are available at most software stores but they can be quite costly. Someone should have a considerable amount of statistical background before attempting multiple regression. There are also a number of other techniques that can be used. Various types of nonlinear regression are available. These procedures assume that the relationship between sales and the spontaneous accounts is nonlinear. Once again, the use of these techniques requires considerable statistical expertise and it is only mentioned here for information purposes.

___ 9 ___

MICROCOMPUTER
APPLICATIONS

The microcomputer has fast become one of the most important tools in the business community. The breadth of its use is limited only to the imagination of the person operating it. As more managers are becoming familiar with the benefits of the microcomputer, their desire for increased knowledge is growing. Unfortunately, in their search many are learning that it can be difficult to find valuable information relating to their needs. It is widely acknowledged that tedious, repetitive work can be made more accurate with the use of a computer. The manipulation of financial figures is well suited for the microcomputer. However, often it is difficult to know just how to get started. Who is using computers? How are they being used? What resources are available? In this chapter these and other questions will be addressed with special emphasis placed on some of the ways the microcomputer can be used to aid the manager in making financial decisions.

The microcomputer has evolved somewhat since its first appearance. In earlier years, many consumers purchased a microcomputer just to find that it really didn't help them as much as they had hoped or, maybe, were led to believe. They learned that it is not the computer that performs the work, but the software or a computer program that "instructs" the computer. Much of the potential of the microcomputer was just out of reach for the person who didn't have the time or desire to learn to write programs. Some were able to invest this time learning the intricacies of its operation and created custom programs that addressed their specific needs. However, most off-the-shelf programs that were available simply fell short of being considered a convenient tool for the manager.

As the microcomputer consumer matured, so did the machine. Programs were introduced that manipulate numbers with minimal effort on the part of the operator. These programs enable the manager to perform calculations in a fraction of the time they can be done manually. After entering a formula one time, the manager can calculate, in seconds, different effects a decision could have on a business. Once the decision has been made to investigate the use of a micro-computer in business, it can be difficult to piece out the mass amount of infor-mation that can be accumulated. With so many different products available, it in fact can be quite confusing.

Early on in the development of the computer industry, different companies were trying to lead the industry with their own individual products. Unfortu-nately, this generated a lack of standards in the industry and sometimes made it difficult for the consumer to make a "smart" decision. Standards have since evolved, and it is now easier to focus on a product without the fear that it will become obsolete as soon as it is acquired. Basically, there are three areas to investigate when faced with the problem of acquiring a microcomputer system: the software, the operating system, and the hardware.

SOFTWARE AND OPERATING SYSTEM

The software is pretty much the most important of the three since it plays the dominant role in the solution. Remember, it is the software that instructs the computer. Close attention needs to be paid to software and it is for this reason that a detailed discussion will come later in this chapter.

An important point to remember when faced with the task of acquiring a microcomputer is that it is not necessary to be a "technical expert" in computers. Many times, terminology can be slightly intimidating. It is not that important to understand what an operating system is, but whether it is capable of performing at the level required.

There are two major operating system environments from which to choose for the microcomputer: single-user and multi-user. The primary difference be-tween the two is that a single-user operating system program can service only one user at a time, and a multi-user operating system can service a number of users at the same time.

To say that a single-user operating system can service only one user is not exactly fair, however. Doing so would be leaving out a very important option, networks. A network is basically an environment that enables different micro-computers to share resources or files. So in a network system, multiple computers that are connected to each other can be serviced, each running under a single-user operating system. In a multi-user operating system environment, multiple terminals or access points are attached to and controlled by only one computer.

The decision to make when considering an operating system is whether there is a need for a multi-user environment. If not, a single-user operating system such as MS-DOS (Microsoft Corp.) might be preferred. If so, preference might be a multi-user operating system such as XENIX (Microsoft Corp.), or a network system running under a single-user operating system.

HARDWARE

Hardware is simply the computer itself and peripherals. The alternatives when considering hardware are, in many cases, highly personal. It is much like purchasing a car. One person likes a Chevrolet and another likes a Ford. As stated earlier, the options in choice have been made greater by the standardization of the many products available. The key aspect to consider in the choice of hardware is the option of accessory boards that can be added to the microcomputer. Options like color as opposed to monochrome, or the minimum memory requirement as opposed to additional memory. All options need to be taken into consideration. This is an important point because not all option boards work the same on all microcomputers. Much of the guesswork involved with the hardware configuration has been eliminated by the requirements of the software. For instance, a program that requires color eliminates that decision.

However, with all available options, the purchasing decision can be confusing. Maybe the most direct approach for configuring a microcomputer is to start with the software. Most programs specify minimum hardware requirements for operation. However, if a "special" accessory board is suggested, make sure that it has been tested or verified to work with the machine of choice.

A major factor in the decision to acquire a microcomputer for business is what to do with it. It is easy to feel overwhelmed by the task at hand when information resources are difficult to come by. Having already been bitten once, some can make more educated decisions than others because they have the benefit of experience. There are a couple of examples that might provide insight to others in the same situation.

Example 1

An owner/manager of a small retail business realized that a microcomputer could help profits of the business and decided to acquire one. She felt that she was spending too much time in the back room over a calculator and not enough with other responsibilities. Her first move was to go to the local computer store where she explained her predicament. She pointed out that her budget was fixed. The business carried only three employees, including herself. The main reason she was at the computer center was because she wanted to increase profits. She would be the only person working on the computer since she was the only one doing the books. She did, however, want to train one of her employees to perform more management tasks, so this other person might be using the computer as well. Basically what she wanted out of the computer was the ability to store monthly sales figures for each employee and manipulate those figures against expenses. She then wanted to compare the present year's figures against the previous year and forecast into the next.

She felt comfortable that the computer store understood her problem and now owns a single-user microcomputer that is performing to her satisfaction. Her ambition is great, and when time permits she studies the capabilities of her new investment. She has visited the public library where she has found books and magazines that contain valuable information. She has learned of a computer club in her area and has attended meetings where she found other people with the same interests. She is going to attend a computer show with two others in the club, where they have signed up to attend a seminar.

Example 2

The second example concerns the manager of a department within a major corporation. Although most times he has to get approval for projects he undertakes, he controls the department's profit and loss. His problem is not much different from that in Example 1 in that he wanted to increase profits of the department while at the same time increase productivity of the six people that he manages. He knows the power of a computer since he has had access to the company's data processing (DP) department for some time. He was a little disillusioned by the DP department, however, and sometimes felt as though his hands were tied because he had to rely too heavily on them.

He realized that the solution to his problem was a departmental microcomputer. He was fortunate in having a friend in the DP department who had experience with microcomputers. His friend suggested that he look into a multi-user microcomputer. This would allow each person in the department to have access to the computer, utilizing its full power. He envisioned the entire department's business operating off of this one system. Each person could have access to word processing or store his or her own prospect list. This computer could maintain the department's master customer list and manage sales made by the department. And most important, these sales figures could then be manipulated at anytime to learn "to-the-minute" results.

All of this sounded great, but who was going to do it? The manager had plenty of work already, as did each of the six employees; not to mention the technical knowledge required to undertake such a task. Much thought was put into this project and the decision was made that the benefits justified the expense. The manager looked around and found a computer consultant whom he contracted to do an analysis, and with the advice of this consultant acquired a multi-user microcomputer system. He felt comfortable with the results of this consultant, but felt it was necessary to hire a dedicated computer person whose responsibility it was to oversee this project. The department is slowly but surely implementing the insights of the department manager.

It might be helpful to look closer at what is really allowing these people to be so productive. Computer software is the most important aspect of a microcomputer system. It is the software that compares current earnings to previous ones or generates sales forecasts.

SOFTWARE PACKAGES

There are literally hundreds if not thousands of software packages on the market. Many are unique in their results and many are close duplicates of each other. There are, however, categories that help us communicate their function. Probably the most useful for the financial manager would fall under the category of spreadsheets.

Spreadsheet Programs

The spreadsheet program is made up of a grid of cells containing numbers, formulas, or simple words. Cells can interact by storing formulas that manipulate them. Once a formula has been stored, numbers are entered into the cells that the formula utilizes, thereby allowing complicated calculations to be performed. A major benefit of the spreadsheet program is the ease of playing ''what if'' exercises or performing financial forecasting.

Because of the popularity of spreadsheet programs, there are many different types available on the market. Where each might have its own specific decisive features, probably the more popular at the present is Microsoft's MultiPlan (Microsoft Corp.).

Data Base Managers

Another popular program used in the business community is the data base manager or DBM. The DBM is, in its most simple form, a filing program that enables the operator to store data electronically. The DBM is used in applications such as maintaining customer lists or prospect lists—applications that require the storage or manipulation of large amounts of data.

The statement ''in its most simple form'' was made because many of the popular DBMs have a programming environment built-in to them that enables the operator to manipulate the information stored in the data base to greater levels. What makes the DBM programming environment more appealing to many is that often DBM environment languages can be learned more quickly and easily than other non-DBM environment languages. Some of the more popular DBMs available are dBase III Plus (Ashton-Tate), and FilePro Plus (The Small Computer Company, Inc.).

Integrated Software

In many industries, people are striving for compactness and integration of their product. This philosophy is carried over into computer software where a major player is the integrated program. Integrated programs bundle each of the major software categories and package them as one program. Popular integrated programs offer word processing, spreadsheet control, data base management, graphics, and often communications, all as one program.

The popularity of these programs in the business community is because of their versatility. Not only do the individual applications within these integrated packages offer good solutions in the area of office management and financial forecasting, but the graphics capabilities can provide excellent presentation aids. There have been many small businesses that have relied on the power of these integrated packages. As would be expected, there have been any number of integrated programs introduced on the market, all of which have much to offer, but perhaps the most popular has been Lotus 1–2–3 (Lotus Development Corp.).

PUBLIC DOMAIN SOFTWARE

Possibly one of the most overlooked sources of software for the business environment is the vast amount of public domain software. Many programs have been written addressing a specific problem and placed into public domain. Most programs available through public domain are free or carry a small handling fee. Probably the most common way of acquiring public domain software is through on-line information systems such as CompuServe (CompuServe, Inc.) or Dow Jones News/Retrieval (Dow Jones & Co., Inc.). However, public domain software can also be acquired through local computer clubs. The most direct approach to inquire about public domain software might be through a local computer retail store. A Basic program that might aid in the forecasting process is included as Appendix A to this book.

With the many alternatives that can arise, implementing a microcomputer system can be a difficult and time-consuming task. It is important to think through a decision beforehand as much as possible, but too often the time or expertise are simply not available and the only way to get something done is to just do it. A common mistake made, however, is to underestimate the amount of effort that it takes to implement a microcomputer system. It can be easy to overlook the learning curve required for each component that makes up a system. Therefore, it is important to put in as much time as possible on the front end of the project, even if implementation is to be performed in small steps. If the time is not available to invest when designing or implementing a microcomputer system, a computer consultant can help see the completion through. Even though an upfront expense is accrued, a consultant can often save expense by making suggestions that otherwise would not have been considered.

COMPUTER CONSULTANTS

Computer consultants can offer experience, often heading off a problem before it becomes real. Knowing what to look for and where to look are benefits that can save both time and expense. However, when selecting a computer consultant it is essential to establish a good rapport and to feel comfortable that the consultant thoroughly understands the needs of the business. Many "computer people" can interact well with the machine, but it is essential that the consultant communicate his or her expertise to the financial manager.

Chapter 10 lists some cautions to be observed throughout the planning and forecasting process and offers some sources of assistance to the manager.

___ 10 ___

CONCLUSION

After all the territory that has been explored there is little left to cover. However, there are a few words of caution to be offered before putting financial forecasting basics to work. In addition, there are a number of sources of assistance for the manager, which are mentioned in this chapter.

WORDS OF CAUTION

We've explored a number of facets of the planning process and keep stressing its importance. As a matter of fact, in the Alpha-Delta example it was stated that the planning process should not be shortcut. It must be kept in mind, however, that just because the planning process is important a company should not neglect other facets of management to devote time to planning and forecasting. This caution brings a number of other cautions concerning the planning process to mind.

Don't Spend So Much Time Planning That You Don't Do Anything

Think again about the Alpha-Delta example. We said that Alpha didn't do as good a job of planning as Delta. The reason was that Alpha shortcut the planning process; Alpha didn't ask the necessary questions for planning and therefore didn't formulate the necessary strategies. Delta did. To do so, they spent extra time.

Just because a company shouldn't shortcut the process doesn't mean that they should go overboard on planning. A reasonable amount of time should be spent developing strategies, but at some point further efforts simply don't reap enough benefits. At some point in the planning process a strong leader will have to say "enough is enough." Otherwise planners might get carried away and start planning for "everything." If someone gets to the point where they are thinking about what to do if they have to change coffee services, things have gone too far. Think of planning on the grand scale and worry about the small details as they come up.

Once a good planning process is institutionalized in a business, it is usually easier to keep sight of what is to be accomplished and when things are getting off track. If it is the first go-round for planning and forecasting, it is natural at some point to get carried away on trivial details. If that happens, get a grasp on the situation and think of the big picture. It will be easier next year or in the next planning period.

Don't Let Too Many People Bog Down the Process

It is important to touch bases with all the individuals involved in the planning process. It is also important to keep the lines of communication open. Everyone who has anything to contribute should feel free to do so. It would be easy, therefore, to call a planning meeting and let everyone get involved at every stage of the process. If you do that, though, you'll be staging a three-ring circus. If too many people get involved in every step of the process, things will get out of control and bog down.

To avoid such problems, be very specific about identifying every stage of the planning process. Think about the personnel who should have an input into the process at each stage, and the general types of input they may offer. Then think about the best way to channel that input. How much can be accomplished by memo? How much can be pipelined through a supervisor? How much is likely to fall through the cracks? In planning meetings or when asking for input, be cautious about how many people to get involved. There is a definite trade-off involved. Too many people will bog things down, but don't fail to include someone who is necessary to the process. What you eventually decide depends on the individual situation. Just keep in mind the trade-offs.

Don't Let One Person Run the Show

This may sound a trifle strange after the previous statement. It seems obvious that a strong leader must be involved in the planning process and that strong leader must take control in order to keep things from getting bogged down. On the other hand, that leader has to keep in mind that the objective of the planning process is to come up with strategies. The development of these strategies involves brainstorming. It would be counterproductive to discourage creativity of the individuals involved. A leader has to keep a strong enough rein on matters to avoid planning pitfalls, but the rein must be loose enough so that individuals feel free to explore the limits of their creativity. A strong leader is integral to the process, but the whole process is a team endeavor. How best to achieve this delicate balance of course depends upon each individual situation. As in all other aspects, experience helps.

Don't Forget Good Ideas

At the height of the brainstorming process, a lot of good ideas are going to be generated. Some of these ideas are for items that might crop up in the future, some are outgrowths of other ideas, some are infeasible to attempt right now. In other words, lots of ideas might be generated, but some cannot be acheived in the current planning period. Some sort of procedure should be institutionalized to archive these good ideas and some follow-up procedure should be established to trigger reexamination of the archives. Too many times companies forget good plans, good ideas, and sometimes they even redo jobs because they can't remember what they have done in the past.

Don't Forget the Procedures

Good planning is not easy. This is especially true the first time a company goes through the process. Initially a lot of time will be spent figuring out how to achieve the various stages of the process. A lot of time may be spent arguing over how to go about something. There may be several points where someone will say something like "we can't do anything about this until we get that report from Jones." There are pitfalls at every turn. To save some of this frustration in the future, procedures need to be documented. Save information on who attended what meetings, when, what kind of information was needed, and the like. Especially important is to document all those instances when someone says "the next time we do this we need to remember . . . "

Don't Get Too Institutionalized

This is another of those statements that sounds strange after the previous warning. This is another of those delicate balances that must be maintained. Good planners build on the past and also try to avoid the mistakes of the past. On the other hand, a company should never get so institutionalized that it jeopardizes the flow of ideas that should characterize planning. Remember the big picture.

Don't Let Planners Worry Too Much About Accountability

Sometimes it is easy to get lost in the planning process and forget the original objectives. People start getting nitpicky about statements and send out subtle signals to other individuals. Don't be so stringent about the accuracy of statements and similar matters that you get people worrying more about accountability and covering their respective rear ends than the real objectives you're trying to achieve.

Don't Forget That Planning Is an Ongoing Process

Good planning is never really over. Good planners build on what they have already done. Just because all the statements and budget for some period are completed doesn't mean that planning doesn't go on. Keep the ideas flowing, keep the strategies coming, and keep following up on all those good ideas you have already generated.

SOURCES OF ASSISTANCE

There are some sources of information that may be helpful to a planner. The best is probably the American Institute of Certified Public Accountants (AICPA), which can provide the planner with a number of publications helpful in the planning process. Obviously, these are aimed at accountants and not general managers, however. In addition to these publications the AICPA regularly offers courses for members' continuing education. Some of these cover planning. For information on publications and courses contact the American Institute of Certified Public Accountants, Inc., 1211 Avenue of the Americas, New York, New York, 10036–8775.

Universities and colleges may also offer courses related to the planning process. Often business colleges will also offer noncredit courses for executives. Business colleges may also be a source of information for consultants. The Professional Development Institute at North Texas State University, for instance, regularly offers short seminars on planning and forecasting (as well as other topics of interest to the manager). For information about such offerings, contact the Professional Development Institute, North Texas State University, Denton, Texas, 76203.

Marketing research companies can aid in sales forecasting; they may offer some planning assistance; they might also provide some tips on how to find outside planning consultants. Be sure to check on the reputation of any consultant with professional associates before embarking on a relationship with a consultant. Appendix B at the end of the book contains a directory of industry information sources.

____ APPENDIX A: ____

"BASIC" PROGRAM FOR FINANCIAL FORECASTING

```
10   CLS

20  PRINT:PRINT:PRINT:PRINT

30  PRINT TAB(24);"FINFORE, A FINANCIAL FORECASTING PROGRAM"

40  PRINT

50  PRINT TAB(37);"WRITTEN BY"

60  PRINT

70  PRINT TAB(24);"SHARON H. GARRISON AND W. JOE MASON, JR."

80  PRINT TAB(29);"EAST TENNESSEE STATE UNIVERSITY"

90  PRINT TAB(34);"COLLEGE OF BUSINESS"

100 PRINT TAB(30);"JOHNSON CITY, TENNESSEE"

110 PRINT

120 PRINT TAB(18);"You are free to use this program and share it with others"

130 PRINT TAB(15);"so long as it is not modified in any way without the written

140 PRINT TAB(15);"approval of the authors.  This program provides a short cut

150 PRINT TAB(15);"approach to the forecasting of external funding requirements

160 PRINT TAB(15);"and the calculation of proforma balance sheets for the firm.

170 PRINT:PRINT:PRINT:

180 PRINT TAB(28);"PRESS <RETUR> TO CONTINUE";A$

190 INPUT;A

200   CLS
```

```
210 PRINT:PRINT:PRINT:PRINT:PRINT:

220 PRINT TAB(18);"ON THE SCREENS THAT FOLLOW YOU WILL BE ASKED TO PROVIDE"

230 PRINT TAB(15);"INFORMATION CONCERNING THE PREVIOUS YEARS BALANCE SHEET AND"

240 PRINT TAB(15);"INCOME STATEMENT AS WELL AS ESTIMATES OF THE ANTICIPATED"

250 PRINT TAB(15);"PERCENTAGE INCREASE IN SALES FOR THE COMING YEAR. WHEN THAT

260 PRINT TAB(15);"INFORMATION IS AT HAND, PRESS <RETURN> TO CONTINUE"

270 INPUT;B

280 CLS

290 PRINT:PRINT:PRINT:PRINT:

300 PRINT "BALANCE SHEET PREVIOUS YEAR"

310 PRINT

320 INPUT "CASH,$=";DA

330 INPUT "MARKETABLE SEC.,$=";DB

340 INPUT "RECEIVABLE,$=";DC

350 INPUT "INVENTORY,$=";DE

360 INPUT "NET FIXED ASSETS,$=";DF

370 INPUT "ACCOUNTS PAYABLE,$=";DG

380 INPUT "ACCRUALS,$=";DH

390 INPUT "NOTES PAYABLE;$=";DI

400 INPUT "LONG-TERM DEBT,$=";DJ

410 INPUT "COMMON STOCK,$=";DK

420 INPUT "RETAINED EARNINGS,$=";DL

430 CLS

440 PRINT:PRINT:PRINT:PRINT:PRINT:

450 PRINT  "ADDITIONAL INFORMATION"

460 PRINT

470 INPUT "SALES,$=";AA

480 INPUT "NET INCOME,$=";AB

490 INPUT "DIVIDENDS,$=";AC

500 INPUT "COST OF GOODS SOLD,$=";AD

510 INPUT "SELLING & ADMINISTRATIVE EXP.,$=";AE

520 CLS

530 PRINT:PRINT:PRINT:PRINT:

540 PRINT "GENERAL INFORMATION"
```

```
550 PRINT

560 INPUT "INTEREST ON NOTES PAYABLE,%=";GA

570 INPUT "INTEREST ON LONG-TERM DEBT,%=";GB

580 INPUT "TAX ON EARNINGS,%=";GC

590 CLS

600 PRINT "FORECAST"

610 PRINT

620 PRINT "(PLACE MINUS SIGN (-) IN FRONT OF THE NUMBER FOR ANY DECREASES)"

630 PRINT

640 INPUT "CHANGE IN SALES,%=";FA

650 INPUT "CHANGE IN MARKETABLE SEC.,$=";FB

660 INPUT "CHANGE IN NET FIXED ASSETS,$=";FC

670 INPUT "CHANGE IN NOTES PAYABLE,$=";FD

680 INPUT "CHANGE IN LONG-TERM DEBT,$=";FE

690 INPUT "CHANGE IN COMMON STOCK,$=";FF

700 FX = 1 + FA / 100

710 FY = 1 - AD / AA - AE / AA

720 PA = DA  *  FX

730 PB = DB + FB

740 PC = DC * FX

750 PD = DE * FX

760 PE = DF + FC

770 PF = DG * FX

780 PG = DH * FX

790 PH = DI + FD

800 PI = DJ + FE

810 PJ = DK + FF

820 PM = PA + PB + PC + PD

830 PN = PM + PE

840 PO = PF + PG + PH

850 A = DL

860 B = PF + PG + PH + PI + PJ

870 C = AA * FX * FY

880 D = PH * GA / 100 + PI * GB / 100
```

```
890 E = GB / 100

900 F = 1 -  GC / 100

910 G = 1 - AC / AB

920 FG = F * G

930 H = PA + PB + PC + PD + PE

940 R = (H - A - B - FG * C + FG * D) / (1 - FG * E)

950 CLS

960 PP = PN - R - PO - PI - PJ

970 PQ = PN - R

980 R = INT (R):PA = INT (PA):PB = INT (PB):PC = INT (PC):PD = INT (PD):PE = INT
 (PE):PF = INT (PF):PG = INT (PG):PH = INT (PH):PI = INT (PI):PJ = INT (PJ)

990 PM = INT (PM):PN = INT (PN):PO = INT (PO):PP = INT (PP):PQ = INT (PQ)

1000 LET A$ = "                          $###,###"

1010 LET B$ = "     CASH             $###,###      ACCOUNTS PAYABLE  $###,###"

1020 LET C$ = "     MARKETABLE SEC.  $###,###      ACCRUALS          $###,###"

1030 LET D$ = "     RECEIVABLES      $###,###      NOTES PAYABLE     $###,###"

1040 LET E$ = "     INVENTORY        $###,###"

1050 PRINT TAB(20);"EXTERNAL FUND REQUIREMENTS"

1060 PRINT

1070 PRINT USING A$;R

1080 PRINT

1090 PRINT TAB(24);"PROFORMA BALANCE SHEET"

1100 PRINT

1110 PRINT USING B$; PA, PF

1120 PRINT USING C$; PB, PG

1130 PRINT USING E$; PD

1150 LET F$ = "         TOTAL_____$###,###                    TOTAL_____$###,#
##"

1160 LET G$ = "    NET FIXED ASSETS$###,###     LONG-TERM DEBT    $###,###"

1170 LET H$ = "                                 COMMON STOCK      $###,###"

1180 LET I$ = "                                 RETAINED EARNINGS $###,###"

1190 LET J$ = "                                     SUBTOTAL___$###,###"

1200 LET K$ = "                                       EFR_____$###,###
"
```

```
1210 LET J$ = "                                        SUBTOTAL___$###,###"
1220 LET K$ = "                                         EFR_____$###,###
"
1230 LET L$ = "          TOTAL ASSETS_$###,###          TOTAL_____$###,###
1240 PRINT
1250 PRINT USING F$; PM, PO
1260 PRINT   "
1270 PRINT USING G$; PE, PI
1280 PRINT USING H$; PJ
1290 PRINT USING I$; PP
1300 PRINT
1310 PRINT USING J$; PQ
1320 PRINT
1330 PRINT USING K$; R
1340 PRINT
1350 PRINT USING L$; PN, PN
1360 PRINT
1370 INPUT"    DO YOU WANT A HARDCOPY OF THIS REPORT(Y=YES,N-NO)PRINT=";D1$
1380 IF D1$ = "Y" OR D1$ = "y" GOTO 1400
1390 IF D1$ = "N" OR D1$ = "n" GOTO 1720
1400 CLS:PRINT:PRINT:PRINT:PRINT:PRINT:PRINT:PRINT
1410 PRINT TAB(18);"STANDBY FOR PRINTOUT"
1420 LPRINT:LPRINT:LPRINT:LPRINT:LPRINT:LPRINT:LPRINT:LPRINT:LPRINT:LPRINT
1430 LPRINT:LPRINT:LPRINT:LPRINT:LPRINT:LPRINT:LPRINT:LPRINT:LPRINT:LPRINT
1440 LPRINT:LPRINT:LPRINT
1450 LPRINT TAB(20);"EXTERNAL FUNDS REQUIREMENT"
1460 LPRINT USING A$; R
1470 LPRINT TAB(24);"PROFORMA BALANCE SHEET"
1480 LPRINT
1490 LPRINT USING B$; PA, PF
1500 LPRINT USING C$; PB, PG
1510 LPRINT USING D$; PC, PH
1520 LPRINT USING E$; PD
1530 LPRINT
```

```
1540 LPRINT USING F$; PM, PO

1550 LPRINT

1560 LPRINT USING G$; PE, PI

1570 LPRINT USING H$; PJ

1580 LPRINT USING I$; PP

1590 LPRINT

1600 LPRINT USING J$; PQ

1610 LPRINT

1620 LPRINT USING K$; R

1630 LPRINT

1640 LPRINT USING L$; PN, PN

1650 LPRINT:LPRINT:LPRINT:LPRINT:LPRINT:LPRINT:LPRINT:LPRINT:LPRINT:LPRINT

1660 LPRINT:LPRINT:LPRINT:LPRINT:LPRINT:LPRINT:LPRINT:LPRINT:LPRINT:LPRINT

1670 LPRINT:LPRINT:LPRINT

1680 CLS:PRINT:PRINT:PRINT:PRINT:PRINT:PRINT:PRINT:PRINT:PRINT:PRINT

1690 INPUT "  DO YOU WANT ANOTHER COPY(Y=YES,N=NO)?=;E1$

1700    IF E1$ = "Y" OR E1$ = "y" GOTO 1400

1710    IF E1$ = "N" OR E1$ = "n" GOTO 1720

1720 CLS:PRINT:PRINT:PRINT:PRINT:PRINT:PRINT:PRINT:PRINT:PRINT:PRINT

1730 INPUT"                    TURN OFF MACHINE AND REMOVE DISK";MM

1740 END
```

APPENDIX B:

SOURCES OF INDUSTRY INFORMATION

Dun & Bradstreet
Three Century Drive
Parsippany, NJ 07054
(800) 526–0651

Robert Morris & Associates
P.O. Box 8500 S–11140
Philadelphia, PA 19178
(215) 665–2850

Standard & Poor's Corp.
25 Broadway
New York, NY 10004
(212) 208–8702

Quarterly Financial Report
U.S. Federal Trade Commission
6th Street & Pennsylvania Avenue, NW
Washington, DC 20580
(202) 326–2100 locator
(202) 326–2180 info

U.S. Industrial Outlook
International Trade Administration
14th Street & Constitution Avenue, NW
Washington, DC 20230
(202) 377–2000 locator
(202) 377–3808 info

Survey of Current Business
U.S. Bureau of Economic Analysis
1410 K Street, NW
Washington, DC 20230
(202) 523–0693 director
(202) 523–0777 info

INDEX

ABOUT THE AUTHORS

SHARON HATTEN GARRISON, an Associate Professor of Finance at East Tennessee State University, has published extensively in such journals as *The Financial Review, Academy of Management Journal*, and *The Journal of Portfolio Management*. Dr. Garrison is active in small business consulting and presents seminars to bankers, medical professionals, and small business owners.

WALLACE N. DAVIDSON, JR., currently holds the Burton R. Risinger Chair in Finance at Louisiana Tech University. Dr. Davidson has published over 50 articles in regional, national, and international journals, including *The Journal of Financial Research, The Financial Review, Academy of Management Journal, The International Journal of Management, The Journal of Risk and Insurance, The Journal of Portfolio Management*, and *The Financial Analysts Journal*.

MICHAEL A. GARRISON is president of his own computer consulting firm. He assists clients in the selection, installation, and implementation of computer systems. He is the author of a multi-user information retrieval software system. He and his wife are editors of the *Journal of Financial and Strategic Decisions*.